THE **GOOD**
THE **BAD**
AND THE *EPIC*

ABOUT THE AUTHOR

David Hofmeyr is an award-winning author of two critically acclaimed Young Adult novels. His debut, *Stone Rider*, won both the prestigious Prix Pépites and the Grand Prix de l'Imaginaire in France in 2016, and was shortlisted for the UK's Branford Boase Award. David also brings over twenty-five years of experience as a marketing consultant, customer experience expert and storytelling specialist.

Visit www.goodbadepic.com and www.davidhofmeyr.com.

THE **GOOD**
THE **BAD**
AND THE *EPIC*

SEVEN **STORYTELLING** CODES
TO TRANSFORM YOUR BRAND

BY DAVID HOFMEYR

Paperback ISBN: 9798884506190
First edition: 2024
Book design: David Hofmeyr

Good / gʊd /

Satisfactory in quality or cuantity.

Bad / bæd /

Not good in any manner or degree.

Epic / ˈɛpɪk /

Extending beyond the ordinary.
Impressive; spectacular; awesome.

For Michael and Dianne Hofmeyr,

my epic storytelling parents.

CONTENTS

INTRODUCTION

*'The most powerful person in the world
is the storyteller.'*

– Steve Jobs

Let's be honest: despite a flood of data, AI, and an army of Influencers, many brands today still force-feed us bilge.

Not just those with limited budgets either, even the behemoths are guilty of churning out communication with an astounding lack of coherence.

But there are a few—the epic brands—that consistently cut through the noise and create genuine engagement.

What's their secret?

They tap into an ancient code that unlocks meaning and emotion like nothing else can. Storytelling.

Think about it. Everything we say and do derives from our primal storytelling roots. It's coded into our culture, our mythology, our identity.

Music is story.

Art is story.

Sport is story.

Politics. Nation. History.

And yes—brands are story.

Successful businesses know this. But then why are so few brands deploying epic storytelling technique to deliver meaning? Well, I think the reason is three-fold:

- **First**, in a crowded market, brands are so desperate to be heard that spectacle often trumps substance, and we forget to treat customers as human beings.

- **Second**, there's an over-reliance on AI and data to inform and craft communication. Data and tech are seductive but often lack actionable insights.

- **Third**, while many brands recognise the power of storytelling, few understand that epic marketing hinges on a code of universal story principles.

Every marketing message *must* have a narrative core for it to stir emotion and feel relatable to us as humans. For it to be memorable and compelling. But the revelation I've come to is that these narrative codes can be applied to *every* aspect of marketing, from a commercial to an email newsletter to a pitch presentation. The same principles apply.

The Good the Bad and the Epic offers an easy-to-use model for you to unleash the ludicrous power of story.

Using a simple framework, we'll apply essential story technique to overcome *any* marketing challenge.

We'll look at some good examples.

Some bad.

And some that have become epic.

We'll unpack the *art* and the *science* of storytelling.

We'll understand how famous authors and Hollywood film directors and screenwriters construct narratives to deliver heart-pounding emotion *and* revenue.

I'll freely admit to being a cinephile and loading the book with movie examples, because Film is the perfect way to show how storytelling and commercial return can coexist. Your brand story can achieve the same balance.

New more than ever, especially with the rapid rise of AI, we need stories to make us feel a sense of wonder. And when we embed narrative structure into every message, we tap right into the human condition.

Don't get me wrong—I'm not an Orwellian doomsayer when it comes to AI. Far from it. As a marketer and science-fiction author, I'm awed by what it can bring to brands.

Take, for instance, the 2024 Orange campaign in France. At first glance this viral sensation appeared to be a highlight reel featuring some of the most celebrated male players from the French national football team. Only it wasn't.

At the midway mark—a reversal.

Those male players were actually superimposed over the bodies of the women's team—a feat achieved with AI.

It was a clever reveal that reframed audience perspectives and underscored how skilful women players are.

And it's a prime example of how AI can be used to tell a bigger, more impactful story.

Brands that excel at storytelling always have the edge.

Regardless of the latest technology.

Don't lose out to them.

The Good the Bad and the Epic is packed with everything I've learned about storytelling from over 25 years as a brand marketing consultant, as well as writing my own novels published in more than ten languages and optioned for Film.

My goal is to help you clearly communicate why *your* brand is uniquely positioned to meet your customer needs—and do it more effectively than your competition.

How?

With razor-sharp, relatable stories that will engage your customers and make your brand unforgettable.

Storytelling will always be—by *far*—the finest method for delivering meaning, purpose, and connection.

Simply put:

If you want to *create* and *keep* customers ...
If you aim to communicate with more impact ...
If you're looking to make your brand epic ...

This book is for you.

CHAPTER ONE

The Problem with Marketing

*'Learning to choose is hard. Learning
to choose well is harder. And learning
to choose well in a world of unlimited
possibilities is harder still.'*

– Barry Schwartz

In October 2019, Samsung (in partnership with BBH,
London) reached for the stars. And fell short.

Samsung's website invited people to upload a selfie
photograph of themselves, promising to turn it from an
Earthbound Selfie into a Space Selfie.

The launch was replete with red carpet stars. This was an
event that had garnered serious PR attention, after all.

Why?

Because it coincided with a giant leap forward—the 50th
anniversary of the moon landing.

The idea was to make consumers feel they were part of
something bigger than themselves.

It didn't land.

In his 2019 polemic bemoaning the state of marketing
in *Campaign*, Jules Ehrhardt expresses it perfectly:

'*Here Samsung inserts itself with "Look at me!", a selfie, an act of narcissism. Samsung sullied Space!*'

Marketing stunts and gimmicks might spark interest, but without a narrative core, these attention surges fade. People want brands to wow them with spectacular advertising and make them feel intense emotions. But brands fail to make an impact when they present a situation or event and call it a story. Taking a selfie in Space is a *situation*.

Not a *story*.

Brands are so feverish to compete for attention today they pour millions into making noise. Look at the recent backlash to Jaguar's *Copy Nothing* rebranding commercial, which featured an outlandish group of androgenous-looking young people in colourful outfits swirling around without a sense of purpose, or a car for that matter. If more marketers spent half their time crafting meaningful brand stories for their customers, rather than chasing hype—we'd see stronger connections, greater loyalty, and more sales.

Yes, hype builds awareness but without meaning, or an emotional core, brand messages are forgotten.

But let's cut Jaguar a break, being revolutionary and a bit strange is in their DNA. The ad might not appeal to me, or any car-mad Jaguar fans, but the brand *is* at a tipping point. Either it appeals to a younger audience, or it faces extinction. Plus, given they don't yet have a product, the ad is really a teaser advert. With any luck a story-led ad is coming soon.

And let's cut Samsung a break too. Sure, the Space Selfie might have gone down like a lead balloon, but what brand hasn't fallen to Earth in their marketing endeavours?

And Samsung marketing does sometimes soar.

I'll submit a story-driven ad about a flightless bird at the chapter close, and we'll examine how it drove engagement through adhering to core narrative codes.

But first I'd like to address four words that for me define the current marketing age better than anything else.

A PARADOX OF CHOICE

Decisions are demanded of us everywhere we go. Any visit to the local supermarket—online or brick-and-mortar—will deliver the same monsoon of brands hectoring us:

ADD ME TO THE CART!
JUST ONE CLICK!
BUY NOW!

The reason behind this urgency is hardly rocket science.
Scarcity drives us to action.
It's the fundamental economic principle behind 'buy while stocks last'. When we feel an option is limited, we tend to be more inclined to purchase.
The media frenzy that we're assaulted with daily sends us chasing butterflies down social media rabbit holes, hunting ever more sensational clickbait.
Researchers say our attention spans are down to eight seconds. *Eight* seconds!
That's outrageous. It's a memory span shorter than a goldfish (*nine* seconds).
In fact, researchers say our attention spans are down to eight seconds.
Eight seconds! That's outrageous. It's ...
Yes.
You get the drift.
Hot today, gone tomorrow, that seems to be the trend.

However, that eight-second statistic released in 2015 was later proved dubious. Just think about how many of us binge-watch great television shows, or podcasts, or play story-led video games for hours. Humans have an impressive capacity for attention when delivered through immersion, which comes only through storytelling.

We're all capable of *sustained* attention.

Our problem lies more in *divided* attention.

In his book *Hooked*, Nir Eyal claims that almost 80% of smartphone owners check their device within fifteen minutes of waking up. Every *ping* and *like* demands our attention. Nothing brings this home more than watching commuters doom-scrolling on their phones.

The continual media onslaught we face is an assault on our senses. And it's becoming more extreme.

A paradox of choice can paralyse us and cause us to flit from one brand to another. Worse, it can tie us to a brand that makes no effort to value us simply because it might appear more painful to choose an alternative.

Choice overload doesn't just present problems for every consumer. It's a challenge for marketers and brands. With so many platforms available to publish content, so much data to unravel and so many competitors, brands turn to spectacle and behavioural tactics, like impressions of scarcity.

But yelling 'BUY NOW!' won't pass muster.

Brands today must have a dual focus on profit *and* purpose. They must give us a reason to engage. They must create value and meaning. Stand for something. Be memorable. Help us. Safeguard us and secure our data. Integrate brand experience with customer experience.

All while building sales.

That's a huge amount for a modern business to master. It's why the most epic brands turn to a sure-fire fix.

And no, it's not AI.

A CORNUCOPIA OF AI

The problem with this 'horn of plenty' that AI promises—
and, once again, I recognise the value of AI when used to tell
a bigger story—is that it often negates the most crucial
element of any endeavour: *doing* the work.

Undoubtedly, AI can write a more precise book than I
can, and it will certainly produce it faster than me, we can
agree on that at least. But will the book be *better*?

The true value of writing a book doesn't lie solely in the
finished product, but in the *process* itself.

The value of the work *is* the work.

It's about the journey of research, the study of other
authors, the layering in of personal experiences that have all
brought depth and authenticity to the product.

AI has an astounding capacity to dazzle us. But it can also
strip a message, a brand experience, or a book of its true
value the way a piranha strips it's meal of flesh.

Leaving a clean-picked perfect skeleton.

Without a beating heart.

Yes, AI can draft a faster, more precise, more informed
essay or even a book like this one. But where is the value in
arriving at the answer so effortlessly?

Nowadays we want the view, but not the climb.

That's dangerous.

Sure, a Bot might reach in seconds what takes me years.

But who cares?

The value lies in the journey to the answer.

The effort that goes into the *work*—that's where you find
magic. It hides in the false starts and the failures. Like a story
itself, the journey is where the real insights are revealed.

A GLUT OF INFLUENCERS

Influencer—a person who can sway the opinions and the purchasing decisions of buyers. Who wouldn't want Taylor Swift advocating for their product to her legion of Swifties?

We know it works. It's been around for a long time, dating all the way back to the 18th century.

When celebrities we trust and like endorse products they sell better. That's the appeal.

But now we've seen the rise of the Instagrammer, the TikTokker, the YouTuber, the Vlogger.

Content creators have turned the media world on its head. Brands have been wooing them in droves, with some gaining wealth and influence, yet others proving short-lived.

Lately though we've seen a decline in their power.

A 2023 study reveals that 90% of consumers no longer trust these Influencers, because we can smell the fakery. We suspect big brands are behind their efforts. And the sheer volume of them has led to saturation, while regulation is catching up. So, should you give up on them entirely?

No. I've seen the right person ignite engagement, like Trainspotter Francis Borgeois, famous for his authentic enthusiasm. A perfect partnership with Gucci and The North Face to promote themes of exploration and discovery.

But I've also seen partnerships sour when Influencers prioritise their own exploits over giving airtime to the brand.

Be selective. Partner with the one that resonates with your brand personality and your audience.

Some Influencers are *good* and produce solid content.

Many though are *bad* and come off as self-serving

And only a rare few—those who care passionately and craft authentic content with a narrative core—are *epic*.

AN ANCIENT NARRATIVE FORMULA

Brands are in business only because customers need them. But many brands today still think in terms of out-dated marketing language like *Conquest* or *Create Demand*.

Instead, brands must *persuade* their customers that they have the tools, insights and solutions to help them.

Aristotle argued in his seminal book on dramatic theory and structure, *Poetics*, that three components are necessary for persuasion to occur. Ethos, logos, and pathos:

- **Ethos (authority).** Ethos is Greek for *character*. It means to convince through credibility. Psychology tells us we listen to people with perceived expertise. Actual knowledge doesn't matter. What matters is how much we *believe* you're an expert. Businesses achieve this by behaving in a trustworthy way and consistently delivering what they say they will.

- **Logos (facts).** Logos is a Greek word for *reason* or *explanation*. The word *logic* is derived from logos. It means to persuade an audience with a rational argument. In marketing and business, we use graphs, charts, and data all the time, finding reason and evidence to bolster our argument.

- **Pathos (emotion).** Pathos is Greek for *suffering*. The word *Empathy* is derived from pathos. It means to persuade by appealing to emotions. Skilful orators like Winston Churchill, Martin Luther King and Nelson Mandela, have always known this. When you stir emotion, you have people's attention.

Aristotle wrote his book on dramatic theory over two thousand years ago, but his ideas still resonate.

Carmine Gallo, author of *Talk Like TED*, studied 150 hours of TED Talks, and discovered startling insights.

One standout was Bryan Stevenson's 2012 talk, entitled: *We need to talk about injustice*, which at the time earned the longest standing ovation in TED history.

When Gallo divided the talk into Aristotle's three modes of persuasion—ethos, logos, and pathos—he found this:

- 10% fell under *ethos* (building credibility)
- 25% fell into the *logos* category (data)
- And a whopping 65% of the talk consisted of *pathos* (personal stories)

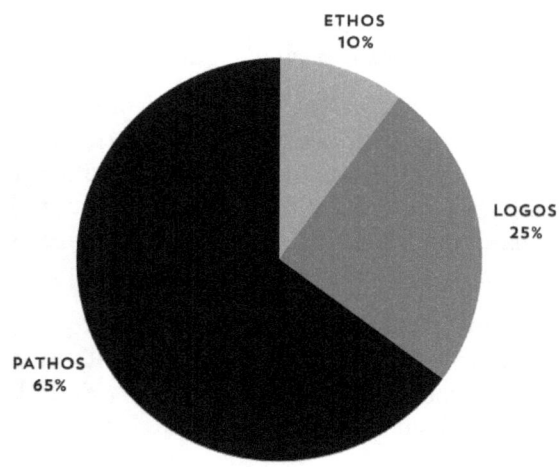

Figure 1: PERCENTAGE OF ETHOS, LOGOS AND PATHOS

Gallo found a startling similarity between all TED Talks that earned the longest ovations and got the most shares. The one thing all these powerful talks had in common was that each speaker was superbly skilled at drawing audiences in with the power of personal stories.

Duke professor Dan Ariely shared the moving story of when he was involved in an accident as a teenager—an accident that left him burned over 70% of his body.

Facebook COO Sheryl Sandberg told a story of her daughter clinging to her leg, begging her not to leave on the morning of her presentation. The story brought home the challenges modern women face in the workplace.

Nothing galvanises like a personal story. It breaks down the walls between the storyteller and us—their audience. It makes us connect with the storyteller's core message and it makes us reflect on our own trials and triumphs.

A personal story is authentic.

It travels like a bolt to the heart.

At the start of this chapter, I showed how giant brands like Samsung, with colossal budgets at their disposal, can still make their marketing efforts go to ground. But when brands apply narrative storytelling technique, and therefore pathos, to their communication, it takes flight.

Samsung's *Ostrich* ad from their *#DoWhatYouCan't* campaign nails narrative structure at its most eloquent.

The ground-breaking commercial, made by Leo Burnett Chicago, opens in the Kalahari Desert, where we see a determined female ostrich strolling away from the flock.

Our intrepid ostrich finds her way onto the porch of a house and comes across a Gear VR headset left behind on the breakfast table. The bird accidentally fixes on the headset and is transported into a new world via a flight simulator.

Fuelled by Elton John's 'Rocket Man' the flightless bird sees what it means to fly. But her attempts at actual flight fail until finally—casting aside the headset and with the flock in admiration and pursuit—she achieves lift-off.

We make what can't be made, so you can do what can't be done, reads the tagline.

The ad ends with a hashtag: #DoWhatYouCan't.

A clever, creative, and entertaining way for Samsung to introduce their Galaxy S8 smartphone and the wonder of VR. And Four Essential Story Elements are here:

1. **The hero with a problem**. The hero ostrich feels different from the flock and clearly wants more from their humdrum desert life.

2. **The guide with a solution**. Under the guise of the Gear VR headset, the Samsung brand enters as a catalyst for change.

3. **The ordeals, trials, and a major crisis**. Our hero ostrich attempts to fly and fails repeatedly, drawing dismay and derision from the flock.

4. **The new plan (that ends in success or failure)**. Our hero commits to her task, throws the headset aside, and achieves what ostriches can't—she flies.

Samsung *Ostrich* is a cinematic example of narrative storytelling. The commercial has won awards at Cannes Lions, The One Show, the Clio Awards, and the D&AD Awards. But … so what? Why does that matter?

It matters because the story engages us enough to watch the commercial through to its conclusion.

It matters because Samsung delivered its message as intended. The *Ostrich* ad successfully conveys the brand's ethos and the product's uniqueness in a way that makes us remember. It works because it follows narrative beats.

It works because it's a *story*.

Not a *situation*.

Elon Musk has built an electric car empire by relying on the controversial mythology of his tweets and his fans—the Teslerati—to do the heavy lifting of his PR. And what is PR, a $100 billion per year industry, but corporate *storytelling*? Using the power of story, Tesla, at the time of writing, has become the most valuable automotive company in the world.

But not every brand has the luxury of a PR machine like Elon Musk, and few brands today have Samsung-sized budgets to throw at cinematic commercials.

Thanks to belt-tightening recessions most brands today have *less* marketing money to spend and are facing tough choices. It's a sobering reality that demands precision. That's why, over the last twenty years, brands have tended to favour performance marketing over brand building.

Performance marketing is defined as paying for results from marketing campaigns—like sales, leads, or clicks—conducted through third-party channels such as direct mail providers, search engines, and social media sites.

Essentially performance marketing is seen as generating revenue in the here and now.

Whereas brand building is seen a long-term investment.

The result?

Many companies have become incredibly successful at performance marketing, but their brands are forgettable.

However, the brands that can find a balance between performance marketing and brand building have better success than brands that favour the former over the latter.

A recent study by Tracksuit and TikTok suggests that brand and performance marketing are BFFs.

The out-take?

More awareness = higher conversion rates.

A brand known by four out of ten consumers is 43% more efficient in driving performance marketing outcomes on TikTok than a brand known by three out of ten consumers.

To fight the headwinds of recession, brands must find a nirvana state between *efficiency* and *effectiveness*. Metrics that measure *efficiency*—ROI, click-through rates (CTR), cost per click (CPC), and conversion rates—are crucial. But story-led brands are *effective* because they deliver the brand *and* customer metrics that bolster performance:

- Awareness
- Trust
- Relevance
- Net Promoter Score (NPS): a customer's likelihood to recommend a company's products or services
- Customer Satisfaction Index (CSI): the degree to which customers are satisfied with a company

Epic brands know this. They turn customers into fans and superfans, not through performance marketing and products alone but through their brand's unique mythology.

Story is a cast-iron way to capture and *hold* attention.

Regardless of budget.

But *why*?

What primordial power does it hold over us? To answer that question, we need to circle back to the very beginning.

CHAPTER RECAP

THE PROBLEM WITH MARKETING

Today, customers skip from one brand to another with impunity. To get and hold attention, marketers will resort to clever *tactics*. But these are often cheap *stunts*. They create a spike of interest that fades quickly. A far more immersive solution lies in narrative storytelling.

Key points to remember:

- **A paradox of choice**. Choice is brilliant but also baffling. Marketers must turn to narrative structure, not cheap stunts, to gain attention. If they don't, consumers will see through the façade.

- **A cornucopia of AI**. Beware the effortless ability of AI to arrive at the answer. The true value of any communication or brand experience lies in the work you conduct to craft the final product.

- **A glut of Influencers**. We're seeing the diminishing power of Influencers. Why? Too much content. Poor regulation. And a declining trust from consumers.

- **An ancient narrative formula**. Narrative structure enables you to grab interest and never let go. In brand marketing, a story—with its emotional beats and engaging cut-through—is proven to be effective.

CHAPTER TWO

Why Storytelling is the Answer

*'The brain desperately wants to make
sense of the world and narrative
structure is the universal format we use
for retaining information in a shareable
and usable form. The PDF file of
human information storage is the story.
That seems to be the mental mode
which sticks the most and gets shared
the most.'*

– Rory Sutherland

Imagine it's a balmy night somewhere in what we now call
Europe. You're sitting at a fire watching flames flicker into
the sourceless dark. Clan faces leap out of the blackness.
Around you float the haunting, hollowed-out melodies of
bone flutes. A log collapses. Sparks whirl up like moths.
Weaving through the smoke, wielding stone spears, the
painted-faced hunters appear. When they drum their feet, a
fever pumps through you. The story of the hunt begins.

Stories reach deep into our past, over 25,000 years.

They're as old as humankind.

These ancient original stories were designed to render us powerless to do anything *but* listen.

Back then your ability to heed the storyteller was key to survival. You *had* to listen to the mammoth hunt to its conclusion. Learning how to hunt, which berries to eat, and which were poisonous, was vital information.

You didn't live long if you didn't listen to the story.

The storyteller would rely on our lizard brains to deliver the most primal emotions. This is the oldest part of our brain—the brain stem, responsible for our survival instincts.

Fight-or-flight? Friend or foe? These are the binary decisions that form the basis of all stories.

The artful storyteller knew this. So, they would load the story with emotion, using empathy to read their audience, and drama to make them cry out, in laughter or fear.

Until something inevitable happened.

Perhaps buoyed by audience reactions, or motivated by a yearning for approval and belonging, they began inventing stories. No longer was it all about conveying the story of the hunt to educate and inform, it became about entertainment and imagination. Invented characters. Made-up stories.

In short … fiction was born.

STORY REVEALS BRAND PURPOSE

Reed Hastings was a day late. He'd rented *Apollo 13* and had forgotten to return it to the giant video chain store on the allotted due date. Back in 1997, this was bad news because it meant a fine. When Hastings got around to finding the DVD, and returning it to the store in Santa Cruz, California, Blockbuster charged him a $40 fine.

Which not only annoyed him but got him thinking.

What if there was a way to avoid fines?

Hastings told the story to his buddy Marc Randolph, and together, they devised a plan that would forever change the way we watch movies at home.

That year, their DVD rental company was born. In 2002, it would shapeshift into an online video streaming service, which ultimately would tip Hollywood on its axis.

The name of the company?

Netflix.

At publication, Netflix has over 270 million subscribers, and its net worth is estimated at over $300 billion—a healthy compensation for the $40 fine in anyone's book. Netflix's rapid success has spawned a horde of fast followers.

Amazon, Apple, Disney, HBO, and ITV are all vying for our attention and our rapacious need for stories.

Netflix represents the trope of entrepreneurial success manifested—**The American Dream**. Two regular people confront a problem. They come up with an original idea to solve the problem that not only makes them sensationally rich but changes the world. Great story, right?

Why?

Because it follows the Four Essential Story Elements:

1. **The hero with a problem**. Hastings is late with his DVD and faces a fine.

2. **The guide with a solution**. Randolph enters the story, and together they make a bold plan to start an online DVD business and avoid fines.

3. **The ordeals, trials, and a major crisis**. They face multiple challenges and go about achieving their goal the wrong way at first (mailing out DVDs).

4. **The new plan (that ends in success or failure).** They adopt a new approach (an online streaming subscription platform) and go on to achieve success.

An epic underdog story gets us all in the gut because it's coded to do that. At some point, we *all* feel like the underdog in our lives, battling overwhelming forces of opposition:

The boss, the bank, the man, whomever.

So, we can all relate.

But there's a catch. The Netflix story isn't true.

It's invented.

Marc Randolph, the co-founder who left the company in 2002, has since conceded that the origin story was fiction to explain why the company was better than its competitors.

They concocted the whole thing. They made it up.

Randolph claims the company began when he and Hastings decided they wanted to create 'the Amazon.com of something'. Shipping DVDs seemed like a neat commercial plan because it filled a gap in the market; customers were willing to buy them online, and—as the two found out by successfully posting a DVD to themselves—they were strong enough to mail. That's it. It's a decent story.

But the Blockbuster one was a belter because it gave us an emotional reason to find them compelling.

Hastings and Randolph wanted their audience to see them fighting for the everyman. It's David and Goliath.

The little guy taking on the giant and winning.

And who doesn't love a story like that?

The Netflix story recalls perhaps the most famous brand origin story of all. Two regular guys build machines in a garage in Los Altos, California, and go on to rule the world.

Two Steves—Wozniak and Jobs—built an empire from their humble garage.

It's a story we all know well—a story that says anybody can do it. We all want to hear that we can make it in life and overcome the odds. It's pure glucose to the soul.

The story caught fire and spread globally.

But here's the thing about that famous Apple story.

That's right. Fabricated. Sure, they spent some time in Job's garage, but maybe a day or two. Wozniak has since admitted that very little work was conducted in the garage.

But that doesn't make for much of a story.

These false origin stories are rife in brand marketing. Fact or fiction, we yearn for stories that move us. According to research by content marketing agency Headstream, 55 percent of consumers are more likely to buy your product if they love your brand's story. Your customers don't require your brand story to be factually correct, but they *do* need it to reveal the truth of your brand—its character and purpose.

So, make them feel something. Be authentic.

Connect to them in a personal way.

When launching the iPod, Apple didn't talk about four gigabytes of memory. Instead, they sought to be authentic, human and personal with this famous line:

Hold 1000 songs in your pocket.

A product proof point is sown neatly into a customer benefit. Humans don't care about gigabytes. We care about music, more specifically, our *own* music. Apple told a story about its product that was all about the customer.

To quote a line from the documentary *Steve Jobs: The Man in the Machine*:

'*The iPod wasn't a machine* for *you. It* was *you.*'

In 2019, when Apple wanted to tell us how great their latest iPhone was at taking photographs, they adopted another powerful storytelling edict:

Show don't tell.

Apple didn't *tell* us about the wizardry of their camera. They *showed* us photographs taken by real people on their iPhones and turned them into billboards that captured multiple stories of human emotion. Their 2019 *Shot on iPhone* campaign beautifully brought to life their brand purpose: *To release the creative soul that lives in us all.*

Ted Levitt, the legendary Harvard Business School marketing professor, famously said:

'*Sell the hole, not the drill.*'

The drill is the product the marketer is selling, but the true value lies in what the drill enables—the hole.

Tap into the problem-solving aspect of the product and you're likely to be more persuasive.

But great marketing goes beyond functional benefits to deeper emotional needs. What really matters is how the hole improves your life and how that makes you *feel.*

Safe. Secure. In control.

Epic brands understand the emotional connections and primal motivations that lie behind the hole.

Coca-Cola doesn't sell soda.

They sell happiness.

Nike doesn't sell sports apparel.

They sell becoming the best athlete you can be.

Apple doesn't sell technology.

They sell the benefit their technology enables: Art. Music. Photography. Whatever creative passion inspires you, Apple empowers. That's the *story* Apple is telling.

A story that reveals their purpose.

In 2017, Larry Fink, CEO of BlackRock, issued a public letter to CEOs emphasizing that 'without a sense of purpose, no company, either public or private, can achieve its full potential.' Brand purpose has evolved from a philosophical ideal to a strategic imperative. Purpose is no longer optional; it's essential for long-term value creation. And nothing builds purpose better than epic storytelling codes.

By focussing on the product's ultimate benefits, Apple applies meaning to its brand. They go beyond the product features to the human story—the *value* the product delivers.

To make their brands matter, Coca-Cola, Nike, and Apple tap into primal emotions: our innate desire to survive, be admired, succeed, love, and protect.

These are the emotions that drive purchase behaviour.

In doing so, these brands become more than brands.

They become cultural symbols.

STORY TRADES IN EMOTION

Legend has it that Ernest Hemingway wrote the world's shortest short story sitting in Les Deux Magots in the sixth arrondissement of Paris. Deux Magots was a café renowned in the twenties as a famous drinking hole for the city's intellectual elite. Hemingway sat at a table with formidable writers: James Joyce, Gertrude Stein, and Ezra Pound.

Being in a bellicose mood, Hemingway announced to all he was about to write the world's shortest legitimate story.

A story in only six words.

Naturally his friends laughed. Undeterred, Hemingway told each to put ten dollars in the middle of the table; if he were wrong, he'd match it. If he were right, he'd keep the pot. Then he quickly scrawled six words down on a napkin and passed it around. Hemingway won the bet.

This is what they say he wrote:

For sale: baby shoes, never worn.

Hemingway is asking us to infer the story. And it's fair to say we can all relate to the emotion and heartbreak in these six powerful words. Hemingway's ability to elicit emotion makes this flash fiction a 'story'. It's *this*—the power of emotion—that makes story such a potent marketing tool.

Because a story, no matter the length, makes us *feel*.

One of the finest examples of making an audience feel is from inarguably one of the best television shows of the last decade. *The Wheel* is the finale of the first season of the brilliant *Madmen*. The show's hero, enigmatic and maverick creative director Don Draper, has a meeting with Kodak to pitch an idea for their new product: 'The Wheel'.

Appealing to Nostalgia over Newness, Draper dims the lights and uses their product to flick through, and linger on, his personal family photographs.

His pitch is deliberate and difficult to forget:

'*This device ... takes us to a place where we ache to go again. To a place where we know we were loved.*'

Nostalgia here is a direct reference to Homer's epic poem, *The Odyssey*. Odysseus yearns for his home in Ithaca and his wife, Penelope. This yearning for home makes his journey more meaningful.

The *Madmen* scene is moving because it's rooted in this ancient mythology and meaning.

STORY STICKS MORE THAN ANYTHING ELSE

Attention-grabbing tactics fly in the face of primal emotion. They might ignite a fireball of interest, but most fade away.

Only by aligning to the core narrative beats can you grab and hold attention. Story—content with a narrative structure, no matter the length—has the unique power to make us feel and *that* cues our brains to remember.

Which brings me to a fact you may soon forget:

'Stories are remembered up to 22 times more than facts.'

Jerome Bruner, a cognitive psychologist, is joined in this view by organizational psychologist Peg Neuhauser, who proposed something blindingly similar:

'*Learning from a well-told story is remembered more accurately and for far longer than from facts.*'

A psychology professor developed a technique that helps the brain retain information. Marty Lobdell, drawing on his experience teaching thousands of students for over forty years, wrote a paper called, *Study Less, Study Smart*. Lobdell set out to demonstrate how much power *meaning* has in aiding the retention of information in the brain.

He conceived an experiment that works like this:

He divides his class into two and tells one group to estimate the vowels in a series of words he reads.

For example, how many vowels are in **mosquito**?

How many in **bottle**?

How many in **elephant**?

The group then writes down what they thought was the number of vowels. Lobdell then asks the second group to rate the *value* of these same items or animals if the students were stranded with them on a deserted island.

The students in this group rate their value on a scale of one to five. Five being high value.

Lobdell then conducts a Stalling Exercise to dump their short-term memory. Then, he asks them to recall the words.

The result? On average, the group counting the vowels in the words remembers around *five* of the 30 words. But the group rating the value of the words, remembers about *10* of the 30 words. A doubling—*that's* the power of meaning.

When you give something meaning it becomes easier to remember. And stories with a narrative core are equipped to deliver value and meaning better than any other method.

We hoard stories in our brains. It's why Rory Sutherland calls story the PDF file of human information storage.

Which means, when we're faced with a surplus of choice, we lean to the brand that leaps to mind first.

The one that sticks—the storyteller.

STORY LIGHTS UP THE BRAIN

Humans are hardwired to react to stories because we've been listening to them since the dawn of humankind.

Without them, we wouldn't have survived.

But there's more to storytelling than its link to our distant past. Stories have a direct impact on the brain.

The stories that move us burn themselves indelibly on our memory. That's because our brains will release chemicals like cortisol, dopamine and oxytocin when we experience an emotionally charged event. This neuro-chemical reaction means that strong emotions *bond* us to a story.

We can watch a Netflix show about Neanderthals, and despite the absence of any Sabre-Toothed Tiger prowling our lounge, we can still *feel* the hunter's terror.

Our brains are equipped with something remarkable.

Mirror Neurons.

Researchers first observed them in studying monkeys. They found that a monkey watching another monkey eat will experience the same brain activity as the monkey doing the eating. It's the same in humans.

We become so immersed we feel the same emotions as the hero in a well-written story.

If they're excited, *we* feel excited.

If they're afraid, *we're* afraid.

Stories even have the unique power to activate parts of the brain that allow us to turn someone else's story into our own ideas and experiences.

It's called **Neural Coupling**.

We assimilate with and *become* the hero.

It makes us feel as if we're living the story ourselves.

That's why horror films like *Joker* and *The Shining* are so chilling: we see the world through the hero's eyes, even when the protagonist is a killer or a psychopath.

Neuroscience tells us why we react the way we do and why stories have such unsurpassed power to make us think something, feel a certain way, and compel us to act.

Marketers are responsible for using this power with care. Brand stories shouldn't be used to 'sell or else', as David Ogilvy once said.

The world has moved on.

Today, marketers must use stories not just to sell products and services but to make us thrive.

STORY CHARTS THE JOURNEYS WE ALL FACE

Joseph Campbell was enthralled with mythology as a young literature professor at Sarah Lawrence College in Yonkers, New York. He was also an avid traveller, in search of meaning in his life and the world. Campbell explored stories, myths, and religious traditions across remote cultures on opposite sides of the world.

And what he discovered was remarkable.

From the Ancient Greeks to the Aztec Empire, Campbell found striking parallels in our stories.

He observed that figures like Krishna, Buddha, and Jesus shared a similar mythological foundation.

Despite vast distances and no contact between cultures, these stories followed the same recurring patterns.

How could it be possible?

To understand this phenomenon, Campbell turned to Psychology. More specifically, Carl Jung's famous theory of the Collective Unconscious—which advances that all human instincts are universally shared.

Campbell used this thinking to propose the idea that every mythic narrative is a variation of one shared story arc.

A concept he called **The Monomyth**.

Within this Monomyth theory, Campbell developed a narrative framework that focuses on the typical stages a hero undergoes in mythic stories.

The Hero's Journey.

A journey comprising three parts:

- A **beginning**
- A **middle**
- An **end**

In screenwriting, these three parts are called **Acts**:

- Act 1: **The Set-up**. We're introduced to the hero.
- Act II: **The Conflict**. The hero crosses into a strange new world and faces opposing forces.
- Act III: **The Resolution**. The hero overcomes the final obstacle.

In 1949, Joseph Campbell introduced the concept of the Monomyth to the world in *The Hero With a Thousand Faces*. Christopher Vogler, a screenwriter and story consultant for Disney, later expanded on his ideas in *The Writer's Journey: Mythic Structure for Writers*.

Vogler mapped 12 plot points onto the three Acts of The Hero's Journey.

These plot points have formed—and continue to form—the roadmap for countless successful Hollywood films.

In the illustration on the following page, you will see how Vogler's 12 plot points map to a **circle**.

The circle is key to the model.

It reminds us that all stories must return to their origin and, in doing so, show the hero's transformation.

We begin the story with the hero not living their best life.

The hero goes through a sequence of trials.

And this journey of overcoming obstacles will deliver the hero to the end of the story—living a better, more prosperous, or at least more *authentic* life.

As I'll demonstrate, it's the same for marketing:

- What transformation are you promising customers?
- What new perception will they gain?
- How will your brand change their lives and the way they behave, think and feel?

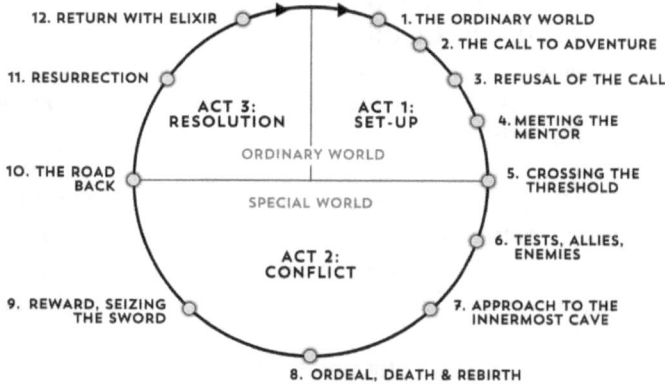

Figure 2: THE HERO'S JOURNEY MODEL

In his 2019 Oscar-winning film, *1917*, Sam Mendes delivers a masterclass, and one of my favourite examples, of storytelling structure. The film conveys powerful emotion because it aligns with the narrative plan we crave.

A resilient soldier must journey across enemy territory—a World War One wasteland—to warn two battalions against an attack that will likely cost 1,600 lives.

A perfect film to unpack The Hero's Journey.

Spoilers ahead!

I'm going to break the story down in detail.

And *then*, I'll show you its marketing relevance:

1. We open on the ordinary world—a green field. Two soldiers, Lance Corporal Blake and Lance Corporal Schofield, rest side-by-side in the grass.
2. They are called to adventure—an order to warn two battalions not to attack the Hun. It's a trap.
3. Our soldiers walk through the trenches and debate their task. This is 'the refusal of the call'. Our hero—Schofield, who will change most—is reluctant.
4. The mentor, a battle-hardened lieutenant gives them advice to get across No Man's Land.
5. They cross the threshold, climbing from the trenches into No Man's Land—leaving the Ordinary World.
6. Now, they are tested. They cut their way through barbed wire and dodge enemy scout planes.
7. They arrive at a bombed-out house—the innermost cave. They drink milk (a symbol of nourishment).
8. At the mid-point, we hit an ordeal—a plane crashes, and they pull a German pilot from the wreckage. Death—the German shoots Blake, and he dies in Schofield's arms. Rebirth—Schofield takes on the mission as his own.
9. The reward—A convoy of friendly soldiers offer to take Schofield part of the way.

10. Schofield crosses a bridge (a literal gateway into the third Act and <u>the road home</u>). A sniper gets him in the helmet, knocking him unconscious.
11. Schofield wakes up—a <u>resurrection</u>. A local girl cleans his wound (bringing him back to life). After which he makes it to the battalions, and he delivers the warning.
12. <u>Return with the elixir</u>—Schofield returns, walks to a lonely tree, and finally rests. Mission accomplished.

Sam Mendes used the Monomyth to drive energy through his story and deliver potent emotional beats.

The structure is his story engine.

Tolkien, Lucas, and Rowling were all influenced by the Monomyth.

Take *Star Wars* and *Harry Potter*:

- Harry and Luke are both orphans living with their aunt and uncle
- A mentor (Hagrid and Ben Kenobi) rescues them
- A villain with family ties (Lord Voldemort and Lord Vader) makes life difficult for the hero
- Both Harry and Luke set out into the unknown, face grave danger and, in doing so, become transformed

Think of *Hamlet* and Disney's *The Lion King*.
Again, we see similarities between them:

- The prince's journey
- The ghost of the father
- The villainous uncle
- The hero's struggle

The Lion King is a reimagining of *Hamlet*, this time with a redemptive, family-friendly outcome.

But the beats of the stories are the same.

Why?

Because their plotlines draw from our global mythology.

Go all the way back to the oldest recorded story of them all, an ancient Mesopotamian poem, *The Epic of Gilgamesh*, and you will find immediate parallels in its structure.

The same is true of modern marketing.

Epic brands, the brands that not only survive but *thrive*, all tell stories. And they do it in a strikingly similar way.

We know stories are a powerful way to beat the noise of a marketplace teeming with competing brands.

We know why stories work and what they do to the brain.

But knowing WHY is not enough.

The key lies in unlocking HOW.

Anyone can tell a great story. It's not some arcane skill that settles on a few. It's accessible to everyone.

All you need is a method—a framework.

In the following chapters of *The Good the Bad and the Epic*, I'll show you how to adopt the same secret formula epic brands use to find millions of fans. They follow a proven narrative approach that works for all businesses.

Unforgettable marketing communication is contingent upon navigating within these narrative borders.

There must be borders for there to be any coherence.

That might sound prescriptive, and rule bound.

It's not.

We've been telling each other stories for over 25,000 years. Stories define us. They make us who we are.

We're biologically wired for brand stories.

The shapes of these stories are native to you as a human.

They beat in your blood.

My goal is to help you awaken your innate story instincts. Not to get lost in theoretical abstraction, but rather to make you aware of the story codes that already lie within you.

The aim is to do it in a way that's as practical as possible. With a simple framework.

To make it easy to apply to *your* brand, I've codified The Hero's Journey into seven storytelling principles.

I call them the **Seven Story Codes**.

CHAPTER RECAP

WHY STORYTELLING IS THE ANSWER

A hurt for sensationalism blunts a brand's ability to connect. But unforgettable marketing lies in unlocking your brand story. Every message you put out there *must* be emotionally bonding. People respond to messages that make them *feel*.

Key points to remember:

- **Story reveals purpose.** Story has the power to reveal the true nature and ethos of your brand.

- **Story trades in emotion**. Data gives stories a boost and credence, but emotion trumps rationality in all decision-making.

- **Story sticks more than anything else**. Stories are more memorable than facts alone.

- **Story lights up the brain**. The human brain pumps chemicals like dopamine into our system when we experience something that's emotionally charged. And *that* cues us to remember.

- **Story charts the journeys we all face**. All stories reflect the transformation in our lives. We go out into the unknown world, and we return having changed.

CHAPTER THREE

The Seven Story Codes

*'For there to be completeness, unity,
coherence, there must be borders.'*

– Susan Sontag

The Good the Bad and the Epic offers an easy-to-follow storytelling framework—a guidebook for crafting marketing communications to overcome any business challenge.

The shape of the framework?

A circle.

Why?

Because all epic stories depict a transformation from one state of being to another.

A journey and a return.

Every well-told marketing story must follow the same Epic Circle pattern. Consider, for example, the typical phases of an automotive customer lifecycle:

1. Discover
2. Purchase
3. Own
4. Renew

Cyclical stories that follow this natural arc are found everywhere in life and in business. And all great marketing stories must comprise **Four Essential Elements.**

These four elements are the fundamental building blocks of all brand stories. Without them you're not telling a story, you're sending messages into the void:

1. **CUSTOMER (the hero) has a problem.** The first stage is about unearthing the story of the hero. In other words, the customer. It's about understanding who they are and defining their *one* core problem and desire, what they want. (Element I).

2. **BRAND (the mentor and guide) offers a solution**. The second part introduces the brand. This covers the brand's role in providing a unique (differentiated) solution and a call to action. The brand must respond to what the customer really *needs*. This is the motivation behind their desire (Element II).

3. **OBSTACLES and a major crisis are faced.** The third stage covers the core conflict, and the ordeals faced by the customer and brand. It must involve a major crisis. Because without a low point, victory is less potent (Element III).

4. **SUCCESS is finally achieved with a new plan.** The brand must partner with the customer and provide an active plan that overcomes the forces of opposition and delivers resolution, and the catharsis audiences crave (Element IV).

Figure 2: THE EPIC CIRCLE—FOUR ESSENTIAL STORY ELEMENTS

The Four Essential Elements fit seamlessly with Campbell's Hero's Journey. The exception is that I break the second Act, where marketing stories can flounder, into two elements, divided by a key turning point—the mid-point.

If the Four Essential Elements represent the bones of all great brand stories, then the **Seven Story Codes** I map onto them are the muscles that keep your story moving.

Drawing inspiration from Vogler's mythic structure, these seven beats are hardwired to improve your brand stories and communications.

It's important to note, that these Seven Story Codes are flexible. They're not rules.

They're *guides*.

Think of them as seven core levers to help you launch ludicrously engaging marketing communication.

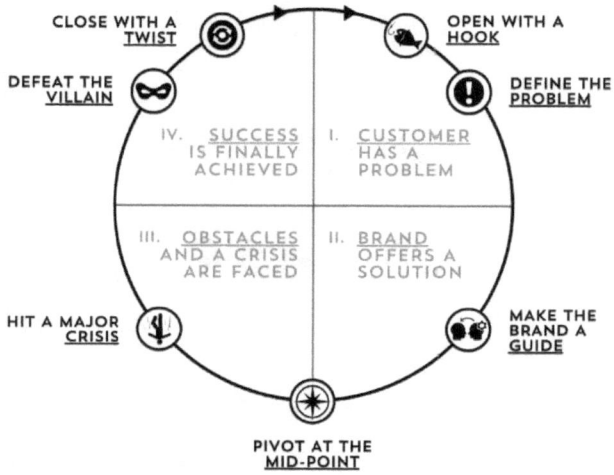

Figure 4: THE EPIC CIRCLE—SEVEN STORY CODES

1. CODE #1—Open with a **Hook**
   The start of a marketing story requires a pledge of something interesting to come. Authors, directors, and screenwriters have always known this. They make the opening sequence count.

2. CODE #2—Define the **Problem**
   In business, the customer is the hero. This means you must develop a deep understanding of who the customer is and use this to demonstrate you that you care about the core problem they face.

3. CODE #3—Make the Brand a **Guide**

   The brand isn't the hero of your story; the brand is the mentor. Your customer has a problem, and the brand must help them resolve it, guide them, and take an active role in creating change.

4 CODE #4—Pivot at the **Mid-point**

   The mid-point of a good story is where we move in a new direction. It should involve an ordeal, a metaphorical death, and the hero's rebirth.

5. CODE #5—Hit a Major **Crisis**

   A low point is crucial. Stories are more satisfying when a hero comes back from the brink of defeat and succeeds. Trust and credibility are earned only when a brand demonstrates that it can help a customer overcome a major crisis.

6. CODE #6—Defeat the **Villain**

   Opposites create conflict and tension, like sparks jumping across the terminals of a battery. Every hero needs a villain. This is the final obstacle that stands in the customer's path. The one thing that holds them back from achieving their goal.

7. CODE #7—Close with a **Twist**

   The final image of a brand story offers a resolution to the customer's problem. The point is to show how the journey has transformed the customer. But the best brand stories leave us wanting more—with a twist that whets our appetite for a new beginning.

CHAPTER RECAP

THE SEVEN STORY CODES

All successful brand stories follow an Epic Circle pattern. A customer has a problem. A brand offers a solution. A crisis is faced. Success is finally achieved. Within this pattern lie universal story principles you can use to plot an unforgettable narrative for any marketing challenge.

Key points to remember:

- **Four Essential Story Elements**. There are Four Essential Elements in every marketing story. These are defined as: Customer Problem, Brand Solution, Obstacles Faced and Success Achieved.

- **Seven Story Codes**. The Four Essential Elements of story incorporate Seven Story Codes. These are proven principles and guides, guaranteed to unleash the ludicrous power of storytelling.

CHAPTER FOUR

CODE #1—Open with a **Hook**

'Start your story as close to the end as possible.'

– Kurt Vonnegut

The start of a marketing story requires a pledge of something interesting to come. Authors, screenwriters, and directors have always known this.
They make the opening sequence count.

THROW THEM OVER THE EDGE

The late great American writer Kurt Vonnegut was a master of narrative structure. His quote, *start your story as close to the end as possible*, is a gem of storytelling advice.

Vonnegut means cut to the chase.

Ignore the preamble. The brain zooms in on action.

So, start running.

An idea exemplified by this famous example:

James Bond (Roger Moore, in a bright yellow jumpsuit) is skiing down a treacherous mountain, bad guys in hot pursuit. Bond, displaying outrageous skill, races down the steep slope, outmanoeuvring them.

Until … a cliff.

Unable to stop, Bond flies over the edge into the void.

All looks lost.

But then he reaches back, pulls a parachute cord and …

Boom!

The chute snaps open, revealing a Union Jack flag.

And we're hit with the famous OO7 theme song.

1977's *The Spy Who Loved Me* hooked audiences right from the start. In Television and Film, they have a name for this sure-fire way to get viewers dialled in from the get-go.

They call it a **Cold Open**.

It jumps us directly into the action. The idea is to get us to emotionally invest in the story as quickly as possible.

Why cold?

Because we come in cold.

No background. No information. No credits or title.

Just straight in.

Modern Streaming shows use the Cold Open to stop us in our tracks and keep us from flicking away.

To cut through the noise, marketers must do the same.

Whether you're writing a presentation or creating a two-minute ad—whatever your marketing challenge—open with something that jolts your audience.

Throw them over the edge.

MAKE A PLEDGE

Apple's logo is lit huge, a planet suspended in space on a colossal screen. The auditorium is buzzing. Steve Jobs steps calmly across the stage of Macworld 2007.

He begins to speak:

'This is a day I've been looking forward to for two and a half years.'

That statement alone draws applause.

One sentence and Jobs has us. It's a **pledge**—a promise of something interesting to come. We're hooked.

He waits. Holds us in thrall.

Then continues:

'Every once in a while, a revolutionary product comes along that changes everything.'

In introducing the iPhone, Jobs knew how to pique our interest and bring us to the edge of our seats.

It isn't the only reason Apple is such a successful brand—and Jobs is hailed by so many as a genius of marketing strategy—but it *is* the *first* principle.

The one that sets everything else in motion.

HOOK your audience.

An effective way to get someone obsessed with your story is to give them an idea of where it's heading.

Great storytellers make everything *appear* predictable from the start. They make audiences eager to find out what happens (even if to confirm their existing ideas).

But here's the trick: the most epic storytellers set our expectations ... and then *subvert* them.

Pixar's Andrew Stanton has an interesting take.

Stanton is the creative force behind many of Pixar's big hits, including *Finding Nemo, Toy Story,* and *Wall-E.*

He's created an equation for making audiences care:

The unifying theory of two plus two.

Through years of storytelling trial and error, Stanton learned that audiences want to work for their meal.

They don't want things handed to them on a plate; they *want* to figure things out.

'Don't give them four. Give them two plus two.'

Give them clues and foreshadowing—enough bait to hook them. Make them anticipate something. Then *twist.*

William Archer, the British Playwright, sums it up in his definition of drama, which he calls:

'Anticipation mingled with uncertainty.'

JJ Abrahams agrees:

'Withholding information ... is much more engaging than offering up the information.'

Steven Spielberg is another master. From the iconic, nerve-jangling theme tune to the mounting threat, *Jaws* keeps us enthralled. In the first half of the film, we barely glimpse the shark. It's a shadowy menace from the deep. This deliberate withholding makes it far more terrifying.

Admittedly, the shark's absence might have been due to budget, but it was a boon for epic storytelling.

The same technique is used by Ridley Scott in *Alien*. The monster reveals itself at the mid-point. Unveiling the alien too soon removes the thrill of 'the unknown'.

You must build up drama, suspense, and tension and release it throughout the story. But the most provocative stories set up the drama from the beginning.

With a pledge.

If you pledge something interesting to come at the start of a story, it works like magic to convince our brains to sit up and take notice. Here is something worthy of our attention. It begs a question that only the resolution of the story will answer. And we're primed to find that answer.

We've all seen advertising that immediately loses our interest. We've all attended a work conference where an amateur presenter points at his first slide and turns his back on us or, worse, taps the microphone and says, '*Is this thing working? Is it on? Can you hear me?*'

Yes.

Do we care? Are we locked in? Are we hooked?

No.

We're bored witless.

Successful marketing campaigns rely on our ability to hold an audience in thrall by beginning with a promise of something interesting to come.

STATE YOUR THEME

Jake LaMotta—portrayed by Robert de Niro—is imprisoned by the ropes of a boxing ring. Flashbulbs pop and die slowly. Black-and-white imagery, with a Cavalleria Rusticana soundtrack, gives the scene a dream-like feel. LaMotta, in the smoky half-light, is a leopard pacing a cage. His slow-motion shadowboxing has a supple, animal quality. He is grace and beauty trapped in muscle and fury.

The question is, who is LaMotta fighting?

It's a question central to *Raging Bull*.

Raging Bull is a story about a boxer struggling to contain his demons within. A man who metes out his rage in the ring. And, beyond it, on those he loves.

It's an opening scene that tells us so much and delivers the essence of the film without a word spoken—this will be a story about a man battling himself.

Who is the hardest opponent we have in life?

Ourselves.

We all know those voices in our heads: the heckler and the hype man. It's a theme tied to some of the greatest films and the most epic brand marketing ever created.

All stories are about the hero's psychological inner struggle. That's the story that moves us and makes us feel something. Directors like Scorsese know this and know they only have seconds to make an impact.

So, they load the opening scene with meaning.

Raging Bull is a masterclass in delivering a potent opening sequence. It's the essence of a story contained in a scene. Hollywood runs on box-office success, so screenplays are codified to guarantee emotion.

Screenwriters know that every story is about one thing—the core message of the story—**the theme**.

Blake Snyder's epic screenwriting book *Save the Cat* introduces 15 beats of storytelling in a three-act structure. His structure is so well-researched that he can offer a recommended script page number to hit the beats. Snyder talks about stating the theme on page five.

In most cases, a minute of screen time represents a script page. So, page five of a screenplay is the fifth minute of the film. The writer must state their theme at the outset.

Right up front.

Page five.

Five minutes into story.

Martin Scorsese used the opening scene of *Raging Bull* to hook his audience, with imagery and music to ignite the senses and evoke his theme.

It's the real story he wants to tell. His message.

And he conveys it from the beginning.

We all know that one friend who can captivate a room with an amusing anecdote or story. For me that person is Patrick Grant. When he's in full flow, he's electric. He's funny, confident, and charismatic. But his real skill is knowing *how* to tell a story—he cares about storytelling conventions.

For example, Patrick is firm in his belief that you must land *one* idea when making a toast.

You raise your glass and say something like:

'Here's to new beginnings.'

That one thing … *that's* your theme.

The best storytellers state their theme early and repeat it multiple times through the narrative, because it's the one message they want their audience to remember.

Steve Jobs understood the power of introducing his theme early and sticking to it.

His central idea at the now-famous introduction of the iPhone in 2007 was the *'reinvention of the phone'*.

A theme he repeated throughout. He used the phrase: *'A revolutionary mobile phone'* multiple times.

He talked about: *'A revolutionary user interface'*.

And *'a leapfrog product'*. That's his theme …

'We're going to reinvent the phone.'

Jobs used it like a thread of steel, running the entire length of his presentation, leaving us with no doubt that this was a product of the future.

Jobs was a master storyteller.

He knew exactly where he was going.

He had a plan and brought his audience along with him, using narrative structure to connect with them.

Jobs never let go of his theme, or his audience.

If you haven't yet nailed down your own marketing or brand story's theme, don't panic. When writing the first draft, authors often have no idea about their theme, and it's only after completing the first draft that a theme reveals itself.

They then rewrite, locking the theme into their story and creating a spine of meaning. Ultimately, you must be clear about whether your theme is already evident in your mind or emerges through the writing.

Every customer communication must have a theme.

Opening with a strong theme hooks an audience.

It tells our brain this is a story worth following.

Apply the same method Martin Scorsese applies to the opening scene of *Raging Bull*.

Distil the essence of what you want to say and release it right from the outset.

Stories must have a purpose—the desired outcome you want to achieve. Your underlying message. Your theme.

Three ways to find your theme:

1. **Start with your customer insight.** The theme of any marketing story is the core message you want to tell. And that's *always* tied to the customer insight. What do they desperately want and why (what's their motivation), and what holds them back from achieving this? Determining this **Customer Truth** will help you discover your theme.

2. **Find your sweet spot.** Starting with the insight, or **Customer Truth**, is a great lens to discover your theme. But it's helpful to layer on two additional lenses to nail the theme. The second is the **Brand Truth**, which is the purpose of the brand. For Apple: *To release the creative soul in us all.* For Nike: *To inspire the athlete that lives in us.* The third lens is the **Product Truth**, often called the **USP** or Unique Selling Proposition. This is the proof-point that will differentiate you. It's effectively the solution to the customer's problem. A phone without a qwerty keyboard was the iPhone USP. A radical USP that delivered a clear theme.

3. **Own the hashtag.** Finally, if you were to create a hashtag for your campaign or presentation, what would it be? By nature, hashtags are short and sharply reflective of the campaign idea. The best hashtags express a concise marketing theme: #LikeAGirl, #BeMoreDog, #DoWhatYouCan't.

INVERT THE PYRAMID

Two seconds. According to Malcolm Gladwell in *Blink*, that's all the time you have for a first impression.

So, pull them in quickly.

Or lose them.

Journalists must do the same.

They know an article must engage readers from the outset because most people read the headline and the opening paragraph, but as the article progresses, there is an increasing drop-off. So, the author must cram the most salient parts of the report into the opening sentence and set the scene with an attention-grabbing context.

An idea called the **Inverted Pyramid**.

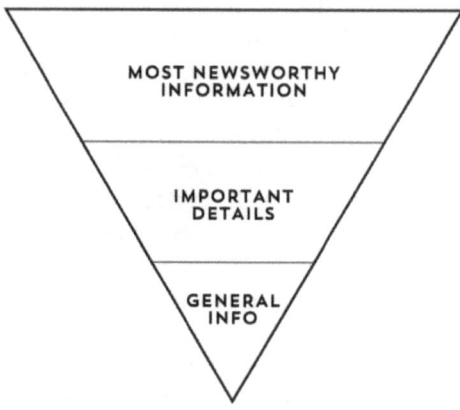

Figure 5: THE INVERTED PYRAMID

The most newsworthy information is at the top of the inverted pyramid. This covers the who, what, when, where, why, and how of the story.

What's the attention grabber?

Be bold.

Be clever.

Be disruptive.

Whatever you do ... don't be boring.

The next chunk of the inverted pyramid is where the writer must expand on the ideas or story elements in their opening salvo and build anticipation.

The final part of the pyramid is the detail. Here, the writer will include the remaining elements of the story.

It's an idea that even works for a campaign email.

Usually, an email's purpose is to drive the reader to the call-to-action button—achieved in three phases.

1. **First**, make people sit up and take notice—grab attention with the customer problem
2. **Second**, build anticipation for your solution
3. **Third**, leave customers eager for a call-to-action

This approach—being provocative right up front—is mostly successful. I say mostly because sometimes, taken out of context, it can fail spectacularly.

This is beautifully illustrated in Burger King's Twitter fiasco of 2021. On International Woman's Day, Burger King UK set out to post a progressive message about their new scholarship programme to help women get a degree in the culinary arts. The aim? To flatten gender disparity.

A worthy cause. But their creative hook was hard-hitting:

Women belong in the kitchen.

Fast followed by the twist:

If they want to, of course. Yet only 20% of chefs are women. We're on a mission to change the gender ratio.

It's clever. It's provocative.
It's *not* boring.
The problem was, few people got past the first tweet and the backlash, to using sexism as bait, was immediate.
The out-take is clear.
Controversial is compelling … but risky.
So, if you're going to be provocative, always test your message first before you put it out there.

BUILD IN IMMEDIATE TENSION

The most brilliant examples of opening with a hook are often found in the first lines of famous books.
The great ones leap off the page and snag us.
Like this belter from James Clear in his international bestseller, *Atomic Habits*:

'On the final day of my sophomore year of high school, I was hit in the face with a baseball bat.'

We're off to a running start. A hard-hitting opening sentence. It's personal and dramatic and it reflects the direct, authentic attitude of the author.
My 2015 novel, *Stone Rider* is a gritty coming-of-age sci-fi thriller set in a post-apocalyptic desert.
It begins in this way:

'Here for blood. Three dark riders. In single file.'

The staccato hit of these opening words evokes the grit of the world. Three sentences, three words per sentence, three riders. *'Here for blood'* is a pledge to the reader. This will be a story of violence, revenge, and bloodlines. Every theme of the book hammers home through the opening sentence—in three words.

Icons of literature achieve the same effect far better than me. Charles Dickens was a master of opening lines.

Perhaps his most celebrated comes from *A Tale of Two Cities*:

'It was the best of times, it was the worst of times, it was the age of wisdom, it was the age of foolishness, it was the epoch of belief, it was the epoch of increaulity ...'

This is just the start of an opening sentence 119 words long. Dickens uses **antithesis**—opposing forces—to set up the conflict of love and revolution to follow.

Barrack Obama famously used antithesis in his address at the Democratic Party Convention in 2004, a speech cited as *the* key factor in his later winning the presidency.

His line?

'There's not a liberal America and a conservative America—there's the United States of America.'

The rhythm of the language and the repetition work here, but it's the opposing nature of his words that powerfully hooks us into his theme. Antithesis is a device that brings tension to a headline or first line of text to draw attention and keep us hooked. Like these examples:

- Feel the **surge** of **calm** (Lexus)
- I'm a **big loser** (SlimFast)
- **Small** seeds generate **big** ideas (CNN)

Sure, these might be slogans and not always opening lines, but the principle is the same. An opening line is powerful when it not only captures the story essence but also introduces immediate tension or opposing forces.

The four pillars of an epic opening line (four Ps):

1. PERSONAL: it has an authentic voice
2. POLARISING: it builds in immediate tension
3. PRIMAL: it evokes a fundamental human need, like survival and self-preservation
4. PROVOCATIVE: it intentionally disrupts, unsettles and unnerves

POSE A QUESTION

Why? Because our brains don't like loose ends. They try to resolve unanswered problems. They want to fill in the gap when we perceive something to be incomplete.

It's called the **Zeigarnik Effect**, named after Soviet psychologist Bluma Zeigarnik, who held that when an activity is interrupted, it may be more readily recalled.

It's why we remember incomplete tasks more than completed ones and why, sometimes, when you're stumped at Wordle and take a break, the answer comes to you lightning-fast when you return to the task.

It's also why questions are a great way to begin.

Headlines that pose a question are difficult to ignore.

The best directors load the opening Act of their epic films with a mystery box of questions.

Who is the main character?

What do they want?

What are they fighting against?

What's the film really about?

Is E.T. about an alien meeting a boy? No. It's really about divorce and how that affects a child.

Finding this out is the magic of the story.

Marketing is no different. Questions prime us to seek answers. They grab our attention and force our brains to fill in the blanks—to seek the truth of the story.

Look no further than one of the most iconic ad campaigns of all time. One that's run for thirty years on a two-word question. In 1993, and for two decades after, this famous campaign, which featured some of the biggest celebrities of the time, dominated the media. More than 350 ads ran nationally in the US, reaching 80% of all US consumers. A campaign so powerful that the California Milk Processor Board even revived it during the COVID-19 pandemic. Talk about longevity and lasting well beyond a peak of interest. 30 years on, a simple question prevails.

Got milk?

****

First impressions matter. Whether crafting your opening line of copy, giving a presentation, or delivering a pitch, you have seconds to make an impact.

That's why the first code of *The Good the Bad and the Epic* sets everything else in motion.

And it's perhaps the most important of all.

Open with a HOOK.

Make your audience take an immediate interest. Hack through the noise. Start running. Get people to sit up.

At a pitch, that's everyone in the room watching you.

For an author, it's the reader.

For a director and screenwriter, it's their film audience wide-eyed in the dark.

And, for a brand and business, it's **the customer**.

CHAPTER RECAP

CODE #1—OPEN WITH A HOOK

It's a simple idea. Hook them or lose them. The start of any message must immediately pull audiences into the brand or product story you're telling.

Checklist:

☐ **Have you thrown your audience over the edge?** Do you drop them right into the middle of the action with a Cold Open that cuts to the chase?

☐ **Do you make a pledge to the audience or the customer?** Have you set expectations high and made a promise of something interesting to come?

☐ **Is your theme stated?** Have you identified the central idea of your brand communication, the *one* thing you want your audience to remember?

☐ **Have you inverted the pyramid?** Have you loaded the opening lines of your email, webpage, or presentation with the most salient information?

☐ **Have you built in tension?** Have you woven a tension-filled insight into your opening line?

☐ **Have you posed a question?** Does your opening pose a question that compels us to read on?

CHAPTER FIVE

CODE #2—Define the **Problem**

*'More than anyone Odysseus codified
the long-term, mainstream
understanding of "hero"—one who
suffers, one who endures, one who
survives a long and complicated
journey through dangers and perils,
and thereafter emerges with his honour
and identity intact.'*

– Lee Child

In business, the customer is the hero.
This means you must develop a deep understanding of who
the customer is and use this to demonstrate that you care
about the core problem they face.

MAKE THE CUSTOMER THE HERO

Too often, businesses frame an objective for what the brand needs to achieve—increased awareness, sales, engagement, loyalty—rather than beginning by thinking about the customer and what will ultimately benefit *them*.

A business-first ambition statement ignores customer needs and considers *only* what the business wants.

This is often written as a **S.M.A.R.T. objective**:

- **S**pecific
- **M**easurable
- **A**ttainable
- **R**ealistic
- **T**ime-bound

So, a business-first ambition might read:

How can we cut costs in two years by decreasing traffic to our call centre and driving traffic online?

A fair question.

It has all the attributes of a S.M.A.R.T. objective and clearly articulates the business problem.

But it doesn't consider this in a human-centred way.

The objective fails to reflect the issue the customer faces.

It merely imposes a business will on them.

By reframing the question to be human-centred, we place the customer at the centre of the ambition.

To do that, you must first *understand* your customers:

- What do they want, that they may not currently be able to achieve—what's their **goal**?

- What's behind this—what's their **motivation**?
- What's holding them back—what's the **conflict**?

Let's imagine additional research reveals that customers become most frustrated with your brand when looking for a quick response to an issue after purchase but have no idea where to go for answers. A reframed question might read:

How might we make our customers feel we care about them when they have a product issue immediately post buying but don't yet know where to turn for an answer?

The question flips to focus on the customer.
It puts the customer first.

In storytelling, a problem facing the hero or protagonist is known as a **Central Dramatic Question.** It disrupts the Ordinary World and sets the hero out on a journey.

A brand experience or communication must start with a customer problem posed as a question.

And the question must never invoke a solution.

A good way to guard against this is to delete the word *by*.

For example: 'How might we get customers to adore us *by* doing XYZ.' No good. You need the central question to spawn *many* ideas. Don't have a solution already baked in.

Your goal is to know as much as you can about your customer and to make their core problem your question.

Let *that* drive multiple solution ideas.

In business, your brand endures by helping customers.

By putting them at the centre of your ambitions.

Your brand is not the hero.

The hero is the customer.

In the late nineties, Steve Jobs returned to Apple as an advisor and drove significant changes. Most people didn't understand what he was doing—brought into sharp focus when a question, loaded with contempt, was directed at him at the 1997 Worldwide Developer Conference at Apple Park in Cupertino, California.

The conference was packed full of developers. And developers have an instinctual loathing of marketers who, for them, talk incessantly about things like feelings and values and have limited awareness of facts. A view no doubt held by the developer who demanded this:

'*Mr Jobs, you're a bright and influential man ...*'

Laughter rippled through the audience, visibly bolstering his confidence.

'*It's sad and clear,*' he added, '*that on several counts you've discussed, you don't know what you're talking about. I would like, for example, for you to express in clear terms how, say, Java in any of its incarnations—addresses the ideas embodied in OpenDoc.*'

A few caustic and derisive words later, the developer sat back down, and the crowd shifted excitedly.

Jobs sat in contemplation. Then said this:

'*You've gotta start with customer experience and work backwards to the technology. You can't start with the technology and try to figure out where you're gonna try to sell it ... As we have tried to come up with a strategy and a vision for Apple, it started with what incredible benefits can we give to the customer. Where can we take the customer? Not starting with sitting down with the engineers and figuring out what awesome technology do we have and then how can we market it.'*

Start with the customer and work backwards to the technology—a groundbreaking idea back then.

20-plus years on, it's become mainstream.

Amazon.com founder Jeff Bezos admits he is passionate about customers. He maintains that putting the customer first is critical to their success. Of which we can agree, they've had a little. Amazon's annual revenue is more than $575 billion (as of publication). Bezos even goes so far as to insist on having an empty chair at every company board meeting. According to Bezos, the chair represents the most critical person in the room. The customer.

Putting the customer at the core of your business means you place *their* needs at the centre of everything you do.

Every customer is essential.

Every touchpoint they have with your brand—in-store, online, or in life—is significant.

Every interaction has the potential to erode or strengthen your brand.

That's why modern CEOs fixate on making the customer the hero and doing everything they can to understand them.

But this is key to all stories and all marketing …

A well-told story has *one* hero.

ONE.

Even a multi-character epic like *The Avengers* has one hero. Who is it? Iron Man.

How come?

Well, Tony Stark undergoes the most change.

His arc is the heartbeat of the story.

Marketing is no different.

Pick a hero for your campaign—the person whose life you aim to positively change.

Your customer. Your design target.

Be specific.

Not women aged 40 to 60, but Rebecca, 51, a divorced mother of four. Have a clear image of her in your head. Understand her needs. It's *her* arc that matters.

If you target everyone, you're likely to miss the mark.

Target the one, not the many.

And be clear about what that person wants.

CLIMB INTO THEIR SKIN

Companies that believe their brand is the hero ask:
How can we improve things for us?

Enlightened companies ask:
How can I make things better for the customer?

It's a question that begs *empathy*.

Empathy is the only way to develop solutions to improve a customer's life. You need to ask probing questions and carefully observe the person answering, their body language and gestures, to understand what they want.

Because here's the problem:

People *don't know* what they want.

Customers can easily describe a problem they have, but not the best solution.

This is an idea made famous by Henry Ford (although the validity of the attribution is dubious):

*'If I had asked people what they
wanted, they would have said faster
horses.'*

– Henry Ford (Allegedly)

The point here is self-evident. Customers would never have thought of a car with four wheels since they had no idea this was the new technology they craved.

That's why I talk about *creating* and keeping customers. Great marketers don't just answer the needs of existing customers—they create *new* customers by finding product experiences that people had no clue they needed.

There are many examples of this:

- The motorcar
- The touch-screen smartphone
- Even extra chunky spaghetti sauce (watch Malcolm Gladwell unravel this in his 2004 TED Talk, *Choice, Happiness, and Spaghetti Sauce*)

As a marketer, you're able to build brand experiences and communications that matter to people only when you listen to their needs with empathy.

When you climb into their skin.

And see the world through their eyes.

To attract customers, you must ask the right questions and analyse the data to understand their desires.

But here's the catch:

What people **Desire** …
Is different from what they **Need**.

FIND THE LINE BETWEEN NEED AND DESIRE

Finding the balance between Need and Desire, and catering to both, are guaranteed to be the jet fuel that launches any story from blah to brilliant.

These two components are crucial to understanding the central character in any story.

Whether for entertainment or business.

- **DESIRE** is a character's external goal: this is their objective, and it drives the momentum of the story. It's evident to the hero and *explicit*.

- **NEED** is a character's internal goal: the lesson they will learn that lies at the emotional core of the story. It's hidden from the hero and *implicit*.

In *The Anatomy of Story*, John Truby elaborates:

'Desire is a goal ... on the surface. But Need is the key to the whole story, and it remains hidden.'

Gravity deals with a scientist stranded in the vacuum of Space after a mid-orbit destruction of her Space Shuttle.

The desire line of the story is an explicit objective: for the hero, Dr. Stone, to survive and get back to Earth.

This is the central question:

Will she survive and make it back to Earth?

A central question always reflects the hero's desire line.

Tarantino's *Kill Bill* is a classic example—with a central question tied to the film's title:

Will the bride kill Bill?

A clear desire line allows a story to maintain focus. The point is to give audiences something to follow.

In *Gravity*, we want Dr. Stone to get back to Earth. This pulls us through the story (like gravity pulls a stone to Earth).

The same logic prevails in marketing.

Customers should have a clear desire line—something they want that the brand can help them achieve.

Three aspects of a strong desire line:

1. **You only want** *one* **desire line**. This must build steadily in intensity, or the story will fall apart. It's the same in marketing. Think about the one core goal your customer has. Then, develop and deliver your unique solution to *that* one problem.

2. **The desire should be specific**. Truby says the more specific, the better, which makes perfect sense in marketing. We must know what success looks like for the target audience. Knowing the specificity of the desired outcome makes the roadmap of solutions and services for the customer much easier to follow.

3. **The hero should accomplish their desire only near the end of the story**. Every good story moves us inexorably towards the end goal. If the hero achieves their desire too early, the story falls flat. The desire line must pull us to the final resolution.

A strong desire line is crucial. But a story will always flatline if it doesn't delve into the hero's *Need*.

Need is key to the character's emotional journey.

And the hero is usually unaware of their need.

In *Gravity,* Dr. Stone's need stems from the trauma that's holding her back—the thing restricting her from living a full life. She blames herself for a freak car accident that killed her daughter. Her self-imposed guilt has driven her away from connecting with people. This is physically manifested by choosing the cold vacuum of Space over Earth.

Here she floats, in limbo, trussed up in a spacesuit and a helmet, utterly removed from humanity.

- **DESIRE** (external goal): to return to Earth
- **NEED** (internal motivation): to let go of her guilt

LETTING GO is *Gravity's* theme.

This is the message repeated by veteran astronaut Matt Kowalski (George Clooney).

As mentor, his role is both functional ...

And emotional.

At the surface level, his job is to help the hero get back to Earth (Desire) by giving her skills, tools, and advice.

But his real job is an emotional one.

To help her let go of her guilt (Need).

This mentor role and purpose is echoed in marketing by the role of the brand. It's seductive to consider your brand or product as the hero in your story. But it's a mistake.

The brand is the mentor.

Not the hero.

Need and Desire is core to every marketing story.

The customer, or the hero, wants something—and this **Desire** is motivated by an unconscious **Need**.

However, multiple conflicts stand in the way and must be overcome before the hero can attain their goal.

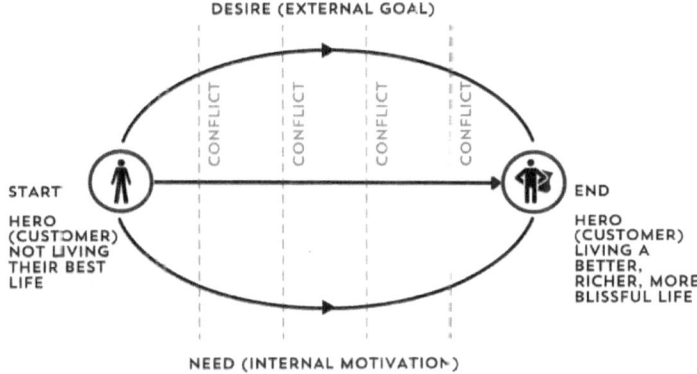

Figure 6: THE LINE BETWEEN NEED AND DESIRE

In marketing, the brand (the mentor) gives the customer (the hero) the tools to overcome these conflicts and achieve their goal. The essential story elements are clear:

1. A customer (hero / protagonist) has a problem. They are struggling to attain a more prosperous, more blissful life. Their desire (external goal) is driven by an unconscious need (internal motivation).

2. The brand (mentor) arrives to help them.

3. The brand gives them tools and advice to overcome any obstacles.

4 The customer finally achieves their external and internal goals (Desire and Need).

To unpick this for your brand, let's select the most accessible story form in marketing—a TV commercial.

If you recall, Samsung's *Ostrich* commercial tells the story of a female ostrich finding a Samsung VR headset and using it to learn how to fly. So, we have:

- **A HERO.** The female ostrich with wanderlust living among her flock.

- **A PROBLEM.** She's bored and wants to escape— an inferred problem. It's never overtly stated, but it *is* implied by her wandering away from the others. She seeks individualism.

Finding the VR headset is the *Inciting Incident*—the catalyst moment that alerts her to a world outside her own. Here, she purposefully crosses over the threshold and enters a new world. Her eyes open. Another side of her is awakened, and she sees her limitless potential.

Her goal is now to fly.

A not-so-subtle dig at Samsung's primary competitor, Apple. Samsung is saying: '*Don't follow the herd.*'

Ironically, a credo that echoes Apple's own brand campaign, established years before: '*Think Different.*'

So, what do we have in terms of Desire and Need?

- **DESIRE:** To learn how to fly. This explicit, external goal allows the audience to follow the course of the story logically and progressively.

- **NEED:** To be an individual. Her need to escape the flock and break free of herd mentality is the internal trigger that sets the story in motion. It's implicit—an internal motivation—and hidden from the hero.

The ad ends with the hashtag: # DoWhatYouCan't.
That's the theme.

The ostrich is *us*—and the message is clear: *we're all capable of doing things that feel beyond us.*

A theme that reflects two things:

1. How Samsung sees itself: as a pioneering disruptor
2. What Samsung believes motivates its audience: not being a follower

It works because it demands a universal question.

Which path do we want to take in life: the one *we* choose, or the one *others* choose for us?

Finding the line between *Need* and *Desire* drives marketing that makes a difference in people's lives.

The Desire is about moving the story forward.

The Need and theme reflect the story's purpose.

It's rare that customers know or can articulate what they need, but they often have an idea of what they desire.

We may desire the latest iPhone because it has all the best features. We might rationalise the cost by saying we bought it for the camera. But a *need* for the iPhone might spring from something deeper. Status, for example.

The SCARF Model, introduced by David Rock, argues five needs make us feel psychologically safe:

*   STATUS: our relative importance to others
*   CERTAINTY: our ability to predict the future
*   AUTONOMY: our sense of control over events
*   RELATEDNESS: our sense of safety with others
*   FAIRNESS: our perception of fair exchanges

Needs are motivations that emerge from our Lizard Brains and are tied to our survival instincts, and our stories.

They are primal.

Associated with **Threat** and **Reward**.

An emotional need ultimately drives every purchase:

- Will it threaten me?
- Will it make me feel safe?

Perhaps the most epic example of a brand responding to an emotional customer need comes from De Beers.

In 1999, Advertising Age named *A Diamond is Forever* as 'The Slogan of the Century'.

A slogan and campaign idea that sprang from two factors:

1. **A product truth**: that diamonds are indestructible and therefore a symbol of enduring strength

2. **A customer need**: for love to be everlasting

FRAME THE PAIN

To cut through the marketplace clutter, brands will often rely on what psychology calls **Availability Heuristic**.

It means we place a higher value on things and memories that come to mind quickly and ignore less easily accessed information, even if that information is more accurate.

A heuristic is just a mental shortcut.

We cut to what's quickly available in our minds.

When we see a choice of brand options, we buy the one we know and remember.

The one that made us feel something at some point.

In other words, the brand that uses pathos.

Harvard Business School professor, Gerald Zaltman, claims 95% of our cognition occurs in our subconscious mind. In other words: we go with what *feels* right.

An example of this is how clients choose an agency in an advertising pitch, where multiple agencies compete for an account. The stakes are high. Winning a prestige account can make or break an agency. So, the very best talent is assembled. Weeks later, the teams emerge—bleary-eyed and gorged on pizza—from secret war rooms armed with the one thing agencies covet most.

An idea!

Now, all they must do is sell it to the client.

But six or seven agencies might be in the mix, all aiming to unleash their brilliant ideas on the same day.

Picking a winner won't be easy.

So, what do clients do?

They go with their 'gut'.

When it comes to quick decision-making, clients choose an agency the way customers choose a product—tilting to the one that makes them *feel* something.

It's the same method that adman Don Draper deployed in *The Wheel* episode of *Madmen*.

Making your audience *feel* is epitomised by an ex-Ogilvy strategy colleague of mine, Sarah Blackman. She has adopted a heart-wrenching appeal to emotion called:
Uncomfortable Storytelling.

It's a powerful tool because it works—it wins pitches.

And it doesn't make the brand the hero.

It makes the customer the hero.

It breaks down like this:

You need to frame the problem to sell a solution. The problem matters most to the customer, and therefore, for the client, it should be top of mind. When agencies highlight the problem, clients tend to overestimate how bad it is and then try to resolve it. So, the agency must reveal the problem.

They must **Frame the Pain**.

When a fertility company for women put out a pitch to create better engagement, Sarah began her research by trawling the Internet, looking for real customer stories.

She quickly realised the brand needed to represent its customers better.

Their content was premium, but it didn't feel *real*.

The brand was delivering sanitised content, tone deaf to the heart-breaking reality of these women and the hardships they faced in trying to get pregnant.

Now, this is obviously a 'fertile' area for rich storytelling.

But the brand hadn't gone there.

Their brochureware content offered a diluted impression of the issues.

In contrast, Sarah discovered a trove of stories about real women expressing real pain in online forums and social media. She picked the stories that hurt the most.

Then, she edited them into a film reel.

And, when it came to the pitch, she hit play.

In five minutes, every person in the room was in tears.

Emotion, achieved through story, brought the clients to their knees.

And it won the pitch.

Sarah used drama, pathos, and theatre to frame the pain and open the floodgates for a new business win.

It's storytelling at its most potent.

Find the customer problem and reveal it to your audience unfiltered and raw. Make them feel what the customer feels.

Make them hurt.

Emphasise this by extrapolating the opportunity lost by *not* capitalising on the issue.

Don't tell them what they stand to *gain* by changing how they operate; tell them what they're losing out on.

Turn the problem into a commercial threat.

We're more motivated by loss than gain.

So, turn the customer problem into a commercial threat by showing the net cost of *inaction*.

Hit them with hard numbers.

The finance people in the room will love you.

MAKE THE PROBLEM A CATALYST FOR CHANGE

In every compelling story, something happens that forces the hero to cross a threshold from the world they know into a new and unfamiliar world.

John Truby calls it: **The Inciting Incident**.

Joseph Campbell calls it: **The Call to Adventure**.

Blake Snyder calls this event: **The Catalyst**—which I like. It reminds me of Newton's first law of motion:

'A body will remain in a state of rest or motion unless acted upon by an external force.'

We've all felt it at some point in our lives.

Inertia.

Safe in our comfort zone, unable to change.

Until triggered.

Newton's First Law is a clear way to think about any catalyst in life and every story arc. If nothing happens to the hero, nothing *will* happen to the hero.

Here's how it plays out in examples from cinema:

- The catalyst in *Gravity* is the debris hitting the Explorer—an event that hooks into the action and forces the hero to act.

- The catalyst in *Kill Bill* is the bride getting shot in the church, triggering her revenge plot—to 'kill Bill'—which will sustain us through two movies.

A situation or plot without a catalyst is *not* a story.

Without a catalyst that triggers Bilbo to meet Gandalf, *The Hobbit* would merely have us following Bilbo around as he goes about his business in the Shire.

No adventure.

No dragon.

No conflict.

A catalyst is a person or an event that *confronts* the protagonist in their ordinary, familiar, comfortable world and *forces* them to enter an unfamiliar one.

It's disruptive and momentum changing.

A catalyst works in two ways:

1. The hero's mindset will not shift; nothing will change in their opinions *until* something demands them to re-appraise how they see the world.

2. The hero's physical environment will remain the same *unless* they're forced to make a decision that drives them out of comfort and toward a new goal.

The catalyst forces the hero to act by being both internal (*need*-based) and external (*desire*-based).

A catalyst is a fundamental part of any good plot, and it's a critical step in all marketing stories, because it gets the customer moving in the brand's direction

The customer problem is a catalyst.

Look at our Samsung *Ostrich* example.
What's the catalyst?
It's her problem. She feels stuck in the herd. This is the internal or emotional trigger which prompts her to act—to walk out into the desert alone. And the consequence?
She will discover the Samsung VR Headset.
And *that* will change her life.
In marketing, the catalyst is the problem that sets the customer on a collision course with the brand.
Take the car industry. To compete and win, automotive companies must understand the many pitfalls, pain points, and decisions their customers face when evaluating which brand and model is the right choice for them.
Something personal will trigger their decision:

- A new family addition
- A change in career
- A move to a new home

These catalysts represent a problem, or a challenge, facing the customer—triggering a journey that will bring them into contact with the brand.
Big ideas and big decisions are born from problems.
The problem is a catalyst.
A call to adventure.
And there *will* be consequences—good, bad, or epic.

ACKNOWLEDGE THE REFUSAL OF THE CALL

As a marketing storyteller you are the conductor. Your job is to heighten and release tension. Awareness of this will elevate your presentations and your brand story from good to epic. In a way, epic stories are like music.

They have a **rhythm** and a **tempo**:

- **RHYTHM**. Rhythm refers to the length of time the scenes in your story take. So, how long are you spending on a point or a slide in a presentation? Don't give every slide the same attention. Pause on some. Move quickly through others.

- **TEMPO**. Tempo refers to the activity level within a scene, which translates to *your* energy levels. Too often, presenters give nothing away in the tone of their voice or their expression. Mix it up! Move from low energy to high energy and back.

Story is CAUSE and EFFECT.

Something happens to the hero, and now they must make a decision that will affect the story's outcome.

When the customer meets the brand, they must decide.

Buy, or don't buy?

Click, or don't click?

A decision provokes a customer to pause.

The pause is necessary to *think* about the decision.

But we know that purchases are led by *emotion*.

For many people, a car is the most expensive purchase after buying a home, so we tend to think it's a rational decision. It's *not*. We're not rational creatures.

Arthur Koestler, in *The Ghost in the Machine*, argues that our primitive brain can overpower the rational functions of our evolving brains and result in emotions like hate and anger. Look at the storming of the Capitol Building in the run-up to Biden's Inauguration in 2021. Emotions ran hot that day, eclipsing any logic. This was Lizard Brain behaviour fed by fictional storylines ramped up in media.

When it comes to marketing, the out-take is clear.

Primal instinct drives our first choices.

So, the pause is critical.

It allows us to apply a rational perspective to an emotional response.

- Am I making an impulsive decision?
- Can I afford this product?
- Have I selected the best brand for me?

These questions prompt a 'go, no-go' binary choice.

It's a moment of indecision.

A *temporary* refusal to commit.

Christopher Vogler calls this moment 'The refusal of the call'. The hero always says 'No' to the adventure, at least initially. It works because it makes the hero more *human*.

Humans are habitual animals, and our behaviour is based on defaults—we stick with what we know.

So, change is hard.

And persuading someone to change is harder still.

We're stepping from the known world …

Into the unknown.

Think about new products that throw old behaviours into the dumpster—like shifting from an ICE (Internal Combustion Engine) car to a BEV (Battery and Electric Vehicle). The electric car world is full of the unfamiliar.

Everything is a first: first home charge, first battery issue, first public charge, first over-the-air update. Marketers must acknowledge this complexity that change provokes.

A pause doesn't mean the customer is saying: 'No'.

They're saying: 'Not yet'.

Acknowledging this 'refusal of the call' allows marketers to build in natural moments of reflection.

For example, in CRM, if someone has signed up to your emails before purchase, this is *not* the moment to hit them with a barrage of messages but rather to guide them to information that might answer any doubts.

****

Marketing that leaves a lasting impression and makes a difference in a customer's life doesn't begin with a clever solution; it starts with a problem—something a brand must resolve for the customer in a way no one else can.

Apple, once again, understands this marketing idea better than most brands. They define a specific customer problem and then unlock a particular solution to tackle it.

As in this famous example:

- **Problem**: professional photographers don't believe the iPhone is the best camera.

- **Solution**: @Apple on Instagram shares only product demonstrations from the public with #ShotoniPhone and many are breathtaking.

Every epic brand must do four things:

1. Find out who your ideal customer is and define their problem.

2. Propose a unique solution for them (give them a reason to buy from you).

3. Overcome any challenges that stand in their way.

4. Provide a new path to achieve ultimate success (and beat your competition).

These are the Four Essential Elements that constitute the building blocks of all epic stories.

Thus far in *The Good the Bad and the Epic* we've looked at the first quarter of the framework, in other words we've identified the **customer** and their **problem**.

Now, the **brand** must arrive with a **solution.**

CHAPTER RECAP

CODE #2—DEFINE THE **PROBLEM**

Every brand must know its customers' core needs and desires and demonstrate that it truly understands them.

Checklist:

- ☐ **Is your customer the hero?** Have you put the customer at the heart of your business? Does your marketing objective articulate their goal?

- ☐ **Have you established a powerful customer insight?** Have you looked at the data to see what the customer wants and what holds them back?

- ☐ **Have you climbed into their skin?** Have you invited customers into your thinking? Have you asked for feedback and listened with empathy?

- ☐ **Have you established what the customer *desires* versus what they *need*?** Desires are external goals. Needs are internal motivations.

- ☐ **Have you framed the pain of the customer?** Don't sugar-coat the problem. Stories are more effective when you expose human truths.

- ☐ **Do you acknowledge the customer's problem as a catalyst?** What are the internal and external triggers that force the customer to act?

CHAPTER SIX

CODE #3—Make the Brand a **Guide**

'The ideal gap between the brand image (what customers are promised) and the brand reality (what customers experience) is zero.'

– Matt Watkinson

The brand isn't the hero of your story; the brand is the mentor. Your customer has a problem, and the brand must help them resolve it, guide them, and take an active role in creating change.

BEHAVE LIKE A MENTOR
(BE CREDIBLE)

When Odysseus, King of Ithaca, went to join the Trojan War, he entrusted the care of his kingdom to Mentor, the teacher and overseer of Odysseus' son, Telemachus.

This reference from Homer's epic poem, *The Odyssey*, may well be the origin of **the Mentor**.

Today, to mentor someone means to be their trusted counsellor or guide.

We join mentor programmes to gain learning and advice so that we can elevate our lives.

We seek people who possess attributes like:

1. Empathy
2. Experience
3. Expertise

Likewise, mentorship in business is synonymous with wisdom, teaching, and support.

Joseph Campbell, in his Monomyth model, calls out the mentor as the one who will help the hero on his journey. The mentor's role is to guide the hero towards achieving their goal and help them overcome obstacles.

Theirs is the voice of encouragement and experience.

It's Nike, motivating us to 'just do it'.

Heroes—or *customers*—launched into an unfamiliar world, are impulsive and eager to explore the new world.

But they make mistakes and go about things in the wrong way. The hero needs to gain knowledge and experience of the new world. The mentor does not.

Mentors—read, *brands*—are veterans.

They are the symbolic adults in the story.

So, we find in classic stories that the mentor is often physically older—a wise campaigner:

- Morpheus in *The Matrix*
- 'M' in *Casino Royale*
- Gandalf in *Lord of the Rings*

The list goes on. But age is a metaphor. Mentors just need to be more familiar with the new world, and therefore wiser—i.e. they see the world as it really is. In the M. Night Shyamalan film, *The Sixth Sense*, the protagonist is Bruce Willis' character, Malcolm Crowe. He is the character who will transform most through the story and must navigate an unfamiliar road. He is therefore the 'hero'. The mentor in this case is a young boy. Cole Sear, Haley Joel Osment's character—who lands this famous line:

'*I see dead people.*'

Cole *Sear* (see what they did there?) brings to the story unique expertise, experience, and knowledge. He's familiar with the world of ghosts. Malcolm is not.

Major spoiler alert—Malcolm will only learn what Cole knew right from the beginning. That *he* is a ghost.

An epic twist.

In *Gravity*, the mentor is George Clooney's character, astronaut Matt Kowalski. As a veteran, he is more familiar with the dark vacuum of Space than the hero, Dr. Stone. His primary role in the story, aside from providing levity, is to use his expertise to help Stone, release her guilt over her child's death and find her way back to Earth.

In short, his role is to help her survive by guiding her to confront and understand her true motivations.

The mentor helps the hero understand not only *what* they need to achieve but also *why* they must achieve it.

Your brand has the same responsibility.

Look at any brand in the automotive industry. A vehicle is a complex product—customers *use* it and *inhabit* it.

When you buy a car, you put your trust entirely in the brand. When you hit the brake pedal, you expect that vehicle to come to an abrupt stop. You trust in the brand's engineering and expertise. Your life, and the lives of your family, are in the hands of that brand. You depend on their knowledge to keep your family safe.

That's *what* you're buying.

It's also *why* you're buying.

You expect safety for your family—and you trust the brand to deliver.

In 2007—after 30 years of research on **Trust**—Shawn Burke of the University of Florida found that all models of trustworthiness share three common pillars (the same for business leaders as it is for brands):

- **Competence**. The belief that a person (or brand) has the professional competence to fulfil the job, meet expectations and deliver results.

- **Integrity**. The belief that a person (or product or brand) is telling the truth is being transparent and reliably keeping promises. They 'walk the talk'.

- **Goodwill (benevolence or service to others)**. The belief that a person (or brand) has your best interests at heart and cares about your needs.

This last point about goodwill came to light in an online discussion between Malcolm Gladwell and Ford's President of Americas, Kumar Galhotra.

Their conversation about 'The Future of Movement' inevitably turned to Silicon Valley v. Detroit.

The question for debate was this:

Who will drive the new revolution of autonomy?

Tech companies, eager to compete with Detroit's big guns, have long been rumoured to be developing driverless cars as the 'ultimate mobile device'.

But Gladwell isn't having it. Sure, these tech companies have all the capital and clout. But Gladwell would rather have the revolution come out of Detroit than Silicon Valley.

His rationale?

Silicon Valley has yet to demonstrate that it has our best interests at heart, citing how Facebook has behaved (owning our data without permission).

But when he looks at the traditional automakers—Ford, Chrysler, and General Motors—he sees companies with generations of commitment to the consumer.

For Gladwell, they have proven competence, but above all, he believes they will act in his best interests. Gladwell is placing his trust in the brand archetype of 'the veteran'.

In other words, the MENTOR.

Seth Godin, in *This Is Marketing*, says a brand must:

'Invite an audience on a journey where change might happen. And then, if you've opened all those doors, it has to solve the problem, to deliver on the promise.'

However, changing behaviour is hard because habits, defaults, and social norms drive people.

In other words, we are more likely to choose brands if they align with our existing behaviours, offer a path of least resistance and if other people seem to like them.

Brands overcome these challenges when they behave like a mentor. And all good mentors share three common traits:

1. **They are CREDIBLE**: they are knowledgeable and get the job done
2. **They are TRUSTWORTHY**: they tell the truth and keep promises
3. **They CARE**: they act in the best interest of other people (the hero and the group)

Ingvar Feodor Kamprad was born on 30 March 1926 on a farm in the Swedish province of Småland.

Hard work, frugality, and egalitarianism typified his rural childhood. These ideals became the hallmark of the ludicrously successful furniture company he built.

Everyone's favourite home store giant—IKEA.

The brand's purpose?

To bring affordable, beautifully designed furniture to everyone's home.

But what can we learn from the global success of their self-assembly flat-pack model?

It's a behavioural truth. Now called:

The IKEA Effect.

It means that we value objects more if we have a role in making them. We are willing to pay more for experiences requiring extra work, like assembling furniture, rather than buying it pre-assembled.

This concept is directly related to *The Good the Bad and the Epic* and the role of the mentor.

A mentor's job is not just to present a solution to the hero and then disappear. The mentor must teach by doing.

They must **involve the hero.**

IKEA works so well because they involve us in making the product, which imbues it with value.

However, an argument must also be made for those mouth-watering meatballs at the check-out counter!

When customers actively participate in a brand's products, the products become more valued. But, in the same way the hero shouldn't be passive, the mentor in a good story is never passive either. They don't just offer the hero advice and stand back to watch. They get involved.

In epic stories, mentors help the hero overcome their challenges and open a new world of opportunity for them:

Morpheus teaches Neo how to fight and navigate his way through the Matrix.

Gandalf battles orcs alongside Bilbo.

Dumbledore challenges Harry and his assumptions of what he's capable of achieving.

Mentor brands must do the same. A brand must help customers overcome obstacles to achieve their promises of a better, more prosperous, more blissful life.

But they must also learn when it's right to lean in.

And when to lean back.

When to prompt customers.

When to leave them alone.

We see this in email marketing. The same offer sent at different times can have varying success. An example of this is fines. Prompting those owing Courts Service fines with a text message 10 days before the bailiffs are sent to a person's home *doubles* the payment rate.

Brand CREDIBILITY comes from building trust and actively participating in people's lives when it matters most.

Don't just give them a call to action and a solution.

Help them achieve it.

Give them a plan.

SET EXPECTATIONS AND DELIVER THEM
(BE CONSISTENT)

In 2012, Ogilvy UK won a pitch to redesign the Land Rover website. As the lead planner at the time, it was my job to gather insights and develop a strategic proposition.

First, we reviewed surveys to understand Land Rover customers and their views about the brand. We learned that people loved five things about the brand:

1. **Land Rovers are iconic**: they stand out
2. **They represent the best of British**: a wry humour and a stoic spirit of *keep calm and carry on*
3. **They are built by experts**: the brand is known for its pioneering 4x4 credibility
4. **They fit in anywhere**: an opera house, a desert, or even a brickyard
5. **They deliver power and strength**: Land Rover vehicles have peerless capability

Land Rover is a company that builds beautiful machines that go *Above and Beyond*, traversing the most inhospitable landscapes in the world.

We realised we needed something epic to celebrate this niche *expertise*.

Humans place an enormous value on expertise.

Think about our almost irrational trust in doctors and lawyers. We trust authority figures even when their judgements are sketchy, amoral, or plain wrong.

Look at the Milgram Experiment, which found that 65% of people were okay with administering shocks to people in another room when a man in a white coat told them to do it.

As humans, we *want* someone in control—someone to make the chaos and confusion of life more bearable.

So, we crave brands that consistently deliver expertise and knowledge at the highest quality. This is particularly true of brands that we trust with our safety. And our family's safety. We're dealing with primal needs.

That's what a Land Rover site must acknowledge.

Our proposition?

Passionate expertise.

The idea gave us a point of difference for Land Rover.

It tapped into the brand's psychology and brought to life the passion and depth of knowledge of the people who build and test the vehicles—the ones who make them feel iconic.

And, importantly, the ones that safeguard your family:

- The engineers
- The designers
- The test drivers

We told *their* stories.

Stories that would demonstrate how Land Rover was able to consistently go *Above and Beyond*.

Stories that brought to life the advanced vehicle technology and the passion and expertise of the engineers who built and tested the technology.

Stories that showcased the vehicles' unique capability in extreme desert and mountain landscapes.

Cinematic, immersive stories that demonstrated how the vehicles tackle any terrain.

What set the site apart was that it understood the brand's role in the customer's life. Land Rover has profound and credible knowledge no one else can claim.

The role of the site is to deliver that brand promise of unique experience and EXPERTISE.

And do it with the most irresistible emotion there is.

PASSION.

A brand message, an experience, a product, a service, a website—all these things must resonate with an audience.

Customers want to hear and feel something they've been longing to hear and feel, something they're open to believing. People come to the Land Rover site with all sorts of expectations. They want the brand to live up to the image they've built up in their heads. They want a first impression that meets their expectations.

A psychological reason why we form first impressions is called **Confirmation Bias.**

People tend to find evidence to support their beliefs and ignore the evidence against them. We arrive at first impressions with pre-existing opinions, biases, and feelings. We spend years building up this armour of bias.

Consequently, the deeply held opinions that make up our mythology and worldview are difficult to shake.

Need proof?

Try bringing someone around to your point of view on COVID-19 vaccines or the Israel-Gaza conflict.

It doesn't matter how much reason we bring to the debate; when people believe something to be true (regardless of evidence), they tend to maintain that opinion because it *feels* right. And will say anything to rationalise their view. Which means they seek facts to support their belief and will seldom elevate themselves out of the echo chamber.

The term Confirmation Bias was first coined by English psychologist Peter Wason in 1960, but marketers are still using it to drive sales. Brands can establish potential customers' beliefs and supply them with evidence to support those beliefs. If your company has a strong brand image that people associate with, you only need to *confirm* this when they arrive in your store or land on your website. This is the moment that will define the rest of the brand relationship.

Get it right, and it sets a solid bond.

Get it wrong, and it's difficult to recover.

But how do you confirm someone's belief about your brand? Simple.

Give them what you told them to expect—in the way they expected—and do it again, and again, and again.

It's about PREDICTABILITY.

Whether you see a Disney movie or visit a theme park, you know what you're about to experience—you know what to *expect*. And—in most cases—Disney delivers.

This is a brand that understands its purpose or the reason why it exists in the world. Which, for Disney, is:

To create joy for the young and for the young at heart.

McDonald's follows a similar logic.

On any road trip that passes the Golden Arches, my nephew yells at me to stop from the back seat.

What's the pull of salted fries, a gallon of sugar water and a one-size-fits-all burger dropped into a cardboard box?

Well, precisely that.

My nephew gets the burger he expects and wants when he walks into a McDonald's. He gets what the brand promises on the tin—a drink, a box of fries, and a burger carried out of the kitchen fast and hot, which has the same feel and flavour every day of the week. No more. No less. As he walks through the neon glare of the arches, my nephew is met with an aroma of burgers that makes his mouth water for the familiar. McDonald's, through its marketing and brand legacy, *tells* you what to expect. Its fast-food chains *deliver* what you expect.

McDonald's are only able to meet my nephew's clear expectations because the brand was able to disrupt a stale industry. The first burger joints were not-so-fast, mom-and-pop diners until McDonald's *created* customers they didn't initially have, by completely innovating their burger-making and delivery process and standardising their product.

They *flipped* the burger industry.

The world is changeable.

New technologies, sweeping pandemics, war, economic collapse, and chaos—so many factors can disrupt any existing brand model or success.

That's why you can't just optimise your products and services on what you delivered yesterday.

Past demand is no indicator of future demand.

Brands must innovate to maintain their uniqueness.

The McDonald's brothers worked like Trojans to create an entirely new burger experience that customers today have come to expect as standard.

To be successful, the brand must deliver.

And do it with iron predictability.

Ogilvy UK Vice Chairman Rory Sutherland, whose book, *Alchemy: The Surprising Power of Ideas That Don't Make Sense*, is chock full of wit and wisdom, has this to say on the success of the McDonald's model:

'McDonald's are terribly good at NOT being terrible.'

Rory means their '*absence* of negatives' makes them great. Their burger isn't the world's best …

But they never claimed it would be.

McDonald's mastered the speed and convenience of fairly good burgers. *That's* their promise.

Attracting a new customer costs almost five times more than keeping an existing one.

On top of that, the probability of selling to an existing customer is three times higher than selling to a prospect.

And it takes an average of 12 positive experiences to overcome one negative one.

Customers have so many choices that once they decide a business doesn't understand their needs they move on.

Every lost customer diminishes the value of the business.

But customers *are* still loyal.

Millennials are loyal to brands that offer purpose, convenience and provide meaningful experiences.

Identity nomadic Gen Z consumers, pilloried as the most capricious of all, will stick to the brands they love—the ones they see as both ethical *and* an expression of their identity.

Today, customers call the shots and brands must work harder than ever before to *prove* their value to customers.

They must do *one* thing better than anyone else.

And do it with CONSISTENCY.

LEARN A LESSON FROM A HEDGEHOG
(BE COMPETITIVE)

'The fox knows many things, but the hedgehog knows one big thing.'

In this well-known parable, a fox employs numerous strategies to catch a hedgehog—sneaking up, pouncing, and even playing dead. Yet, every attempt fails.

The reason for this is simple. The spiky hedgehog has evolved to master one thing above all else. Defend itself.

Andy Clark, in his book *The Experience Machine*, says we don't notice standard product attributes; what we notice are the outliers—the bizarrely good things.

Jim Collins, in *Good to Great,* taps into this idea. Collins studied 1,435 good companies and looked at their levels of performance over 40 years, whittling them down to 11 companies that became great. The principle true to all, he refers to as the three circles of **The Hedgehog Concept**:

1. **What you are deeply passionate about**. Good-to-great companies focus on areas that ignite their passion. Nike doesn't just sell sports apparel and running shoes; they have a stake in sport as an ideal. Customers smell fakery a mile away. So, this isn't about finding an area of passion to stimulate, but rather, it's about igniting an *existing* brand passion. It's like the ancient Japanese philosophy of Ikigai— your 'reason for being'. Your Ikigai is your purpose.

2. **What you can be the best in the world at**. This is not about having a high level of expertise. It's about being the *best*—providing products and services no

one else can. When you think about a mentor in great stories, they aren't *pretty* good at the thing that matters most in the story. They are *masters*. Yoda is an absolute master at wielding the Force—the very best in the galaxy. Hedgehogs aren't good at defending themselves. They're exceptional. Beavers build dams like nobody's business. Bees are brilliant at making big, beautiful hives. L'Oréal isn't just *good* at making cosmetics; it's the world's *leading* brand thanks to proven efficacy.

3. **What drives your economic engine**. This is how you intend to generate *sustained* revenue. How will you become consistently the most profitable business in your industry and category?

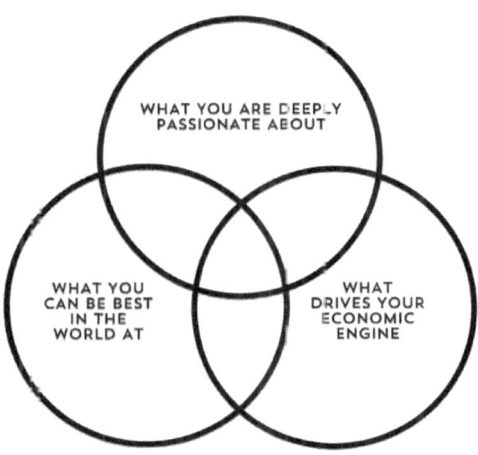

Figure 7: THREE CIRCLES OF THE HEDGEHOG CONCEPT

The Hedgehog Concept is about understanding who you are as a brand and how you compete with others.

What sets you apart?

What makes you hard to kill?

The aim is to define your COMPETITIVE edge in the market segments you're going after and how you can build a strong demand, now and into the future.

KEEP IT SIMPLE
(BE CLEAR)

High-impact, outstanding experiences and solutions offer enormous desirability for customers. But often, we yearn for utility, convenience, and speed—or the path of least resistance. That's one of the reasons why McDonald's is so successful. In a busy world, they keep it simple.

> *'I apologise for such a long letter. I didn't have time to write a short one.'*
>
> *– Mark Twain (Allegedly)*

This quote, attributed to Mark Twain (some claim the quote is much older), says it all.

Being concise requires effort.

It can be hard work.

McDonald's took years of trial and error to perfect their fast-food model. But it's the simplicity of their model that makes it so beautiful.

McDonald's understands that their brand aligns to the Jungian archetype of **The Innocent**. That's the place they want to occupy in our minds. Margaret Mark and Carol Pearson, in their book *The Hero and The Outlaw*, talk about McDonald's restaurants offering '*a clean, well-lighted sanctuary against the uncertainty of modern life*'.

They deliver the same food in the same predictable way, and never confuse customers with too much choice.

It's a reference to Ernest Hemingway's classic short story, *A Clean, Well-Lighted Place*, and reflects an idea that we all yearn to escape the uncertainty of modern life.

McDonald's has that appeal.

They create a temporary Eden—a safe environment, lit by the arches—that offers a reprieve from ambiguity.

As the story goes, in 1504, when Michelangelo was asked how he had created his masterpiece statue of David from a single block of marble, he answered:

'Easy. I chipped away everything that wasn't David.'

The art of great brand storytelling isn't in what you add. It's in what you take away.

Paring back a story and a brand to its core, is critical.

Be ruthless. Reveal the essence.

David Mamet, in his dramatic writing Masterclass, says:

'*Anything in the joke that does not tend toward the punchline kills the joke.*'

It's the same in any brand story.

If it doesn't tend to the punchline, take it out.

Brand experiences and products must be stripped of the superfluous, or risk losing an audience.

That's why Apple's Design Director, James Taylor, talks about the power of **Radical Simplicity**.

Making the product simpler.
And then simpler again.

At the turn of the millennium, Usability Expert Steve Krug published a book called *Don't Make Me Think.*

The book tackles building interfaces that customers can use without any cognitive effort—quickly and intuitively.

For example, websites that parse complex tasks into straightforward actions get better response rates and online sign-up forms are more likely to be completed when pre-filled fields reduce the hassle factor.

When designing a website, the ambition is to get attention fast and drive customers to your call-to-action.

You need to prevent customers from getting lost in the content or frustrated with the interface.

Brevity works across every format.

In *Smart Brevity: The Power of Saying More with Less,* Mike Allen, Roy Schwartz and Jim VandeHei demonstrate the impact of being concise with multiple examples from media. Emails, for example.

The fewer the words, the fewer the ideas and the fewer the calls-to-action, the better the click-through rates.

Three ways to make your emails more effective:

1. Cut your word count dramatically
2. Reduce the number of concepts in your email
3. Include only ONE call-to-action

Do this, and you're guaranteed to get better results.
Keep it simple. Give your customers CLARITY.

****

Brands must offer customers a unique and differentiated solution. They must behave like mentors, guiding customers, helping them achieve their ambitions and, if possible, changing their lives in the process.

The mentor's role is to assist the hero in achieving their goal. Mentor brands must guide the customer by offering expertise and support. In a book this might be a sword or a powerful ring. In business it could be an app, or a product.

Marketers must think about delivering four attributes that allow a brand to answer customer needs:

- CREDIBILITY
- CONSISTENCY
- COMPETITIVENESS
- CLARITY

David Jobber and John Fahy introduced **The Four Cs** in their 2009 book *Foundations of Marketing*.

They are four brand principles that map beautifully to the way mentors behave in powerful narratives.

And who is the mentor?

The brand.

Mentor brands foster connections with their customers by providing guidance, support, and insight.

Rather than focusing on their own achievements, they prioritise the needs and aspirations of their audience and provide a solution to the customer problem.

Which brings me to a key moment in *The Good the Bad and the Epic*.

A point around which your brand narrative must pivot.

The mid-point.

CHAPTER RECAP

CODE #3—MAKE THE BRAND A **GUIDE**

People come to your brand because they have a problem and are looking for a change in their life. The brand's role is to offer a solution and help make change happen.

Checklist:

☐ **Is your brand behaving like a mentor and taking an active role in your customers' lives**? Mentor brands guide and support customers in achieving their goals. Epic brands aren't passive. They take an active role in making change happen.

☐ **Have you set your customer expectations, and are you predictably delivering against them?** Your brand must define customer expectations and then deliver consistently well against them.

☐ **Are you offering a solution or experience that no one else can offer?** Your brand must offer unique experiences and solutions. But being differentiated is not enough. Find a way to be competitive by being the best in the world at one thing.

☐ **Are you making life easy for your customers?** Mentor brands make their products, services, and customer experiences effortless, their ideas simple, and their messages clear.

CHAPTER SEVEN

CODE #4—Pivot at the **Mid-point**

'The heart of drama in any movie is a reversal. You think something is going one way and suddenly everything changes.'

– Rian Johnson

The mid-point of a good story is where we move in a new direction. It will typically involve an ordeal, a metaphorical death, and the hero's rebirth.

CREATE A FALSE VICTORY

At the mid-point of *Mad Max: Fury Road*, Max and Furiosa reach their destination—The Green Place. They've *survived*. At the mid-point of *Gravity,* Dr. Stone finds solace from Space in the ISS. She's *safe*. At the mid-point of the Apple Watch 5 launch video, a girl uses her watch to tear open a portal in the Space-Time Continuum. She's a *superhero*.

These pivotal moments, all at precisely the midway mark, share one thing in common.

They appear to be a victory for the protagonist over the antagonist (the hero seems to defeat the villain).

Max eludes Immortan Joe. Stone escapes Space. And in the case of the Apple Watch 5 commercial, a girl gets the better of her bullies by using her watch to suck them through a portal into another dimension—as one does.

In each case, the mid-point is a **False Victory**.

By that, I mean the hero is offered a respite from danger that may lead them to believe their trials are over.

They are *not*. The stakes will be raised.

The hero will face something that radically changes things and drives them in a new direction. Mid-points, by obvious definition, don't represent the resolution.

They represent an extreme shift or turning point.

No film manifests this better than *Jaws*.

At the mid-point sequence, just when it looks like the hero might win, we see the size of the shark properly for the first time from their boat at sea.

What does the story mentor (Quint) tell the protagonist and hero (police chief, Brody)?

'We're gonna need a bigger boat.'

I love this line.

It delivers the essence of the mid-point.

Sure, it's a testament to them needing a bigger boat to deal with a 25-foot shark, but it really means they need a new plan to succeed. The plot has shifted.

In *Mad Max: Fury Road*, when Max and Furiosa arrive at The Green Place, they believe they've won. But we're only halfway through the story. They quickly see it's not the haven it once was—The Green Place is a dust bowl.

Max now convinces Furiosa to return to the undefended Citadel, which has enough water for everyone. Their journey home is about to begin. The shift at the mid-point here is a shift in goals and a *literal* change in direction—a *reversal*.

The mid-point's role is as crucial in any brand message as it is in any film or book. Unfortunately, few marketers give the moment enough credence. The mid-point plays a pivotal role in the balance of any marketing story. It binds the narrative together. However, the False Victory is the most compelling aspect of the mid-point because it makes the final resolution *much* more satisfying.

This idea applies to any kind of marketing story.

A presentation is a good example.

Obviously, you want the audience to be persuaded by your core message. And what have we established is the best form of persuasion?

Pathos.

Which is to say, storytelling.

An epic presentation needs a narrative structure, and the mid-point plays a key role in that narrative arc.

It's where you must deliver your solution.

The BIG IDEA.

Malcolm Gladwell's 2004 TED presentation: *Choice, Happiness, and Spaghetti Sauce*, is a perfect example of this.

Using humour and story, Gladwell holds his audience in thrall throughout the talk. At the mid-point—10 minutes into his 20-minute presentation—he lands his big idea:

'People don't know what they want.'

Gladwell's entire set up builds to this idea. But he waits until the mid-point for the reveal.
He's building suspense.
If he reveals too soon, he lets the air out of the bag.
Too late? His audience gets exasperated.
You'll see this big reveal often in great films.
When is the first time we see the shark in *Jaws*?
When do we first see the xenomorph in *Alien*?
Yep.
At the mid-point.

Creating a mid-point reveal or pivot can easily be applied to a typical presentation using my Seven Story Codes:

1. **HOOK**: Land the theme of the presentation—be provocative, spark interest, excite your audience.
2. **PROBLEM**: Reveal your target customer's core problem—show an unfiltered customer insight.
3. **GUIDE**: Build the story of how the brand can overcome that problem—the journey you went through to arrive at a solution.

4. **MID-POINT**: Reveal the solution. I often call the middle slide of a presentation THE KILLER SLIDE. If there's one slide that I want my audience to remember, it will most likely fall at the presentation's mid-point. The reason lies in the structural mythology of all stories. There's a tipping

point where you've set up the argument, and now you must hit your audience with the solution. You've generated enough interest to reveal the big idea and then pivot to the second half of the presentation, where you'll bring the argument home. But remember, the mid-point is a 'false victory'. You're introducing something fallible. A *proposition*, not the *resolution*. In other words, you must still test the solution to the limit.

5.   **CRISIS**: Now unpack any barriers. This is where you show your audience you've thought through all potential setbacks. This crisis will win trust.
6.   **VILLAIN**: Outline the new plan to overcome any remaining forces of opposition. The slides here must unpack your development or roll-out strategy.
7.   **TWIST**: Drive your message home and send your audience away with a surprising last thought. End on a high. Leave your audience wanting more.

The first three stages here, or Story Codes, set the presentation in motion.

You're building your argument.

You're saying:

'*Look, we've done our research, we know the customer, and we've learned interesting things about who they are and what they need and desire.*'

But, when you arrive at the mid-point, you need to land your solution in an epic way, and then shift direction.

There's a four-beat flow to this kind of thinking. Four beats that align with the Four Essential Story Elements:

1. **Problem**: start low, with a problem
2. **Solution**: move high with your answer, culminate at the mid-point
3. **Problem**: take them low again, reveal an obstacle, e.g., lack of budget or expertise
4. **Solution**: end on a high, a *new* plan to overcome this issue

This emotional arc is utterly compelling for all audiences because it keeps them riveted to the story you're controlling. The rule, says screenwriting guru Blake Snyder, is this:

It's never as good as you think things are at the mid-point.

Strategic narratives have a shape. Ups and downs. Highs and lows. The story isn't over at the mid-point. It's about to pivot dramatically in a new direction.

Ridley Scott's *Alien* is one of the all-time great examples of this in Film. In the story set-up, a creature attaches to the face of a crew member of the Space tug, *Nostromo*. Later, it detaches and dies. By the mid-point, we assume all is well. It's not. During a final celebration meal—before they return to stasis—we have a reversal. It's bonkers, brutal, and brilliant. A baby alien xenomorph bursts out of the afflicted crew member's chest! Talk about a dramatic shift in direction that follows a false victory. It's easily the most memorable and eviscerating scene of the film.

And it happens precisely at the mid-point.

Bring *this* level of explosive energy and audacity to the mid-point of your presentation. Then veer sharply in a new direction. In all good stories, the stakes are raised immediately after the mid-point, when the bad guys close in. So, as you enter the final half of the presentation, you need to show your audience why the solution might *not* work. You need to punch holes in the argument you have just built.

Sounds counterintuitive, but it works. It's a powerful way to win audience attention and their trust, and it follows the ebb and flow of all great stories. We *want* the rise *and* the fall. We don't want a solution—or the big idea—to be a fait accompli. A solution is only feasible and viable when it has been tested to the limit. And *then* succeeds.

KEEP IT PUNCHY

A story's mid-point is a narrative signpost. Without it, the story can become fragmented. The mid-point reversal prevents the middle of your story from falling into disarray.

It re-invigorates the audience.

Just when their attention might be waning, it makes them sit up. Here is something unexpected.

People get bored quickly—their attention wavers.

And yet, I've often seen presenters attempt to go through a deck with over *a hundred slides*. Barking mad!

Three ways to power-up your presentation:

1. Cut your deck back to no more than twenty slides (this is a rule of thumb, but it's effective)
2. Give yourself forty minutes to present (where your presentation is an hour)
3. Bake in twenty minutes for Q&A

Even at twenty slides—hitting a reasonable average of two minutes a slide—you need to have something impactful at the midway mark, ten slides in. Look around the room at this point—twenty minutes in—at people's faces. You'll see the energy begin to sap. Don't let it happen.

Hit them with a Killer Slide—The Big Idea.

But don't linger long at the mid-point. Move on.

MAKE THE PROBLEM AND THE SOLUTION CLASH

All stories are about a transformation.

- At the beginning of the story, the hero thinks and behaves one way
- At the culmination of the story, the hero thinks and behaves in an entirely new way

This is the basic plot of every great story and marketing narrative. It's the story of how a brand intends to transform a customer's life with products and services.

Brands do that by first understanding their customer's psychological need.

Which is to say, their core problem.

But needs are hidden.

We all shield our true selves.

It's a defence mechanism.

We conceal our doubts, fears, and insecurities. Instead of showing the world our inherent flaws, we portray ourselves how we'd like others to see us. We show them a persona.

A façade that prevents us from living authentically.

A brand's role in marketing is to project that better, more authentic life and help us reach for and achieve that goal. Isn't every commercial ever shot just a visualisation of the promised land—the better version of you?

The most potent marketing stories show how a brand and product will transform a customer's life.

- And turn a problem (e.g. false bravado) …
- Into a solution (e.g. confidence).

In 2019, I had the pleasure of giving an Ogilvy talk on Storytelling alongside BBC screenwriter John Yorke.

One concept in his presentation and beautiful book, *Into the Woods*, blew me away with its clarity.

Yorke has devised a simple model that tackles this dramatic tug-of-war between the hero's problem state (their façade) and the solution state, where the hero can finally reveal their true self (their flaw) to the world.

As the façade falls away, the flaw reveals itself.

Until an inversion occurs.

Where?

At the mid-point.

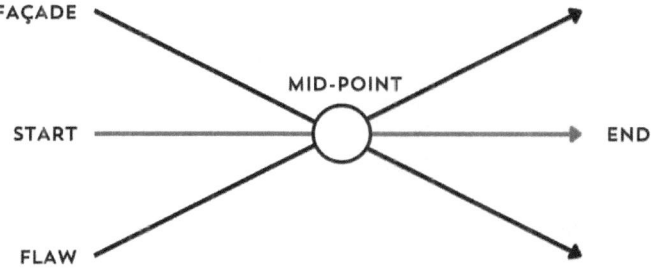

Figure 8: THE MID-POINT IS AN INVERSION

BUILD IN AN ORDEAL, A DEATH, AND A REBIRTH

In The Hero's Journey, Joseph Campbell says the mid-point involves an 'Ordeal, Death and Rebirth'. The mid-point here isn't one moment—it's a sequence of beats.

We can easily see this concept in the film *Gravity*.

Dr. Stone hurtles through Space, lost in a hostile world. Her only ally is the veteran astronaut Matt Kowalski, who uses his thruster pack to rescue her and lead her to the relative safety of the International Space Station.

And we hit the mid-point. The beats are as follows:

1. **Ordeal**. With no air remaining in their thruster packs and unable to stop, Stone and Kowalski slam into the wreckage of the Space Station and get trapped in deployed parachute lines.

2. **Death**. Often symbolic, but here, an actual death. Kowalski sacrifices himself to save Dr. Stone. He unhooks from her and drifts away into Space.

3. **Rebirth**. Stone makes it to a portal and climbs into the abandoned Space Station. She removes her helmet and Space suit (strips down the walls of her façade) and falls asleep, utterly exhausted. Floating in zero gravity, Dr. Stone slowly curls into the shape of a foetus. Wires twist into an umbilical cord. It's a rebirth. She will emerge from this scene galvanised and will take on a more active role in surviving. However, a major crisis is yet to come.

It's the same in any brand story or presentation. The mid-point is where you pivot from the audience's ignorance of the core problem to understanding what they need to do. It represents a rebirth—a new way of operating.

It's *the bigger boat* in the film *Jaws*.

You're showing how your business (or your client's) can be reborn. And take a new approach.

The Ordeal, Death, and Rebirth beats at the mid-point make sense for a two-*hour* film like *Gravity*, but do they apply to a two-*minute* marketing story?

Absolutely.

Returning to Samsung's *Ostrich* commercial (for recall), we see the same sequence.

1. **Ordeal**. Our hero ostrich, transfixed with her VR headset, staggers through the flock, trying to impress them with multiple attempts to fly.

2. **Death**. She leaps high, appearing to begin to lift into the air (a false victory). Instead, she smashes headfirst into the ground (a symbolic death).

3. **Rebirth.** Away from the flock, she searches within to find a new plan (to become an ostrich that flies). Now *she's* leading the flock and they're following behind, running in her wake.

RISE TO A PEAK AT THE MID-POINT

Gustav Freytag was a German novelist and playwright who wrote a book called *Technique of the Drama,* in which he studied the structure of dramatic plays. Freytag found that all great plays have a moment of high drama right in the middle of the story. A climax. Not the story's resolution, but an extreme shift.

He created a simple illustration to bring this to life and it's a powerful reminder of the stake you need to drive into your narrative at the mid-point. It's a tent-pole moment.

A mid-point pivot holds the story upright.

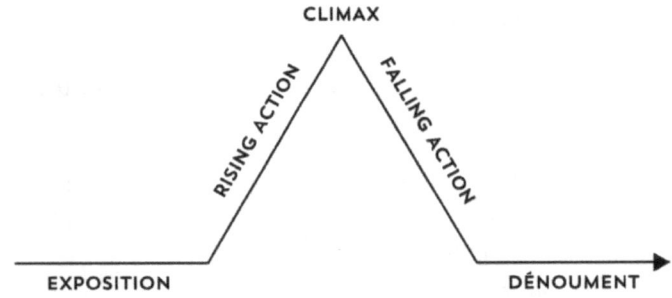

Figure 9: FREYTAG'S PYRAMID

MAKE SURE THERE IS NO GOING BACK

On the coast of Portugal, north of Lisbon, at one of the most westerly points in Europe, lies an unremarkable-looking fishing village with a name that inspires a primal dread.

Nazaré.

Off the shoreline, more than three miles beneath the sea's surface, is a deep rift—the largest underwater ravine in Europe—an ocean canyon 125 miles long.

When the westerly wind whips and the wild Atlantic surges over this rift, monsters rise from the deep—the world's biggest, most notorious waves.

These behemoths have broken backs and claimed lives. Yet, despite their fearsome size and reputation, surfers from around the world come to Nazaré to attempt to ride them.

The Guinness world record for the biggest wave ever surfed was recorded here in 2017. Brazilian Rodrigo Koxa rode an unpredictable 80-foot monster. Put into perspective, that's the height of an eight-storey building.

You can't just paddle out and drop into an eighty-foot wave. It requires help. To achieve an outlandish goal like this, a hero needs an ally. Enter something pioneered in the late 90's that revolutionised big wave surfing.

The jet-ski tow in.

Surfers are pulled out into the waves. And *then* let go.

Which brings me to my point. Riding a monster wave at Nazaré can easily be a metaphor for the structure of any great story. We've got all the component parts

- The hero—the surfer
- The desire—to surf a giant
- The problem, or the need—conquering their fear
- The ally and mentor—the jet ski rider
- The villain—the wave (and the fear it provokes in the surfer)
- We even have a mid-point—not the point where the surfer is halfway through riding the wave, but rather the release from the jet-ski. Everything up to this moment has been a build-up, rising to a peak. The hero and his ally have set out from the beach. They've avoided the pull of the current. They've had a few close calls. But here they are now, a giant wave

looming. They've timed it perfectly. All that's left is for the surfer to let go and find a way to carve down the face. *This* is the mid-point.

Great stories are like waves.

They build an unstoppable momentum.

But there comes a moment, usually right in the middle, where the hero must *commit*. Until this point, things have been happening *to* the hero. The mentor has been pulling them along, guiding them. But at the mid-point, the hero must let go of the leash and strike out independently.

They must take an *active* role in achieving their goal.

Or face carnage.

The mid-point isn't a casual signifier that you're 50% through your narrative. It's a *rift* between who the hero (or the customer) was and who they will become.

To illustrate this idea further, I'll give you an example from the Film industry and then switch back to marketing.

A great Film example comes from a 1972 classic directed by Francis Ford Coppola, starring Marlon Brando and Al Pacino and based on Mario Puzo's novel—*The Godfather*.

Michael Corleone (Pacino) is the protagonist. At the film's start, he presents himself as an upstanding man (his *façade*). He rejects his family's violence as amoral, going so far as to join the army, the opposite extreme of the mafia. But conversely, he's devoted to his father (Brando) and is desperate for his love and respect. And this (his *flaw*, in the story's context) will be his undoing.

At the mid-point of the film, Michael is 'reborn'.

He takes vengeance for his father's shooting.

He murders two men and flees to Italy, where he is protected by *The Family*. The shooting scene happens precisely at the film's midway mark.

Once Michael commits murder, there really is …
No Turning Back.

The second half of the film then becomes about Michael Corleone fully embracing his active role in his new destiny:

Becoming the Godfather.

Francis Ford Coppola's pivot at the mid-point of *The Godfather* is masterful (it also happens to be, in my opinion, Pacino's finest hour).

Can we apply the idea to all forms of marketing?

You bet.

But it's most easily brought to life in advertising, where epic brands cue an audience to believe something is going one way and then redirect them.

A UK brand that does this better than anyone is John Lewis. Their Christmas commercial, *Shadows*, was an immediate hit when it aired in 2007, and it began an unbroken tradition of telling beautifully crafted stories over the holiday season.

Any one of them will move you, but I'll pick *Excitable Edgar* as an exemplar of the 'point of no return' pivot.

At the start of the commercial, we meet Ava, a girl walking through a medieval snow-bound village with her little green dragon friend, the eponymous Edgar (reflecting the brand's partnership with Waitrose). Humour and heartbreak ensue as Edgar attempts to join in on the Christmas action of building snowmen and ice-skating.

But an enthusiastic Edgar breathes fire, and when the ice melts, he ruins the fun.

At the midway mark, the town gathers in the square for an unveiling of their tree. Ava has wrapped Edgar's mouth shut with a scarf to prevent disaster. But this is a false victory. Edgar, unable to contain his thrill, shoots flames from his nostrils and ears. The tree burns to a cinder.

This is the point of no return—the mid-point.

Edgar's failures were mishaps until now, but the tree burning is a calamity. He's ruined Christmas.

There's no going back.

Edgar flees into hiding, and his friend, Ava, plunges into a crisis. She needs a new plan.

I won't give away the end yet, but it's a heart-warming surprise twist with holiday season values.

These 'feel-good' ads create enormous buzz in social media every year. But ... so what?

John Lewis isn't just gunning for a feel-good factor.

They want footfall in their stores.

They want sales.

Do these narrative ads generate profit?

The answer is a resounding *yes*.

John Lewis—despite a financial crisis at the time of their first Christmas commercial, *Shadows*, and when all their competitor brands were still advertising products—took an inspired punt. They invested millions in *story*.

They knew their storytelling—the music, the writing, the mood—had to be precise to convey and 'own' a *feeling* of Christmas. And yes, they succeeded.

John Lewis claims the campaigns '*deliver 20 times the return on their original spend.*'

But they would claim that wouldn't they?

Evidence, though, is hard to ignore.

Independent brand surveys show they achieved a 300% lift in awareness over December, torching the competition.

Even the cover songs in the ads get a sales boost, often hitting number one in the charts. And then there's all the merchandising money from: books, mugs, and toys.

What makes these ads so successful is that they don't feel like ads. There's no product in sight.

John Lewis learned to unlock a method of storytelling to sustain our engagement and grow sales.

They found the dollar and pound value of the narrative structure. And they never looked back.

****

If you don't correctly handle the mid-point of your brand narrative, you're thumbing your nose at the audience.

Don't underestimate how much your audience needs the reveal *and* the reversal. It's baked into our DNA.

A mid-point is the TENT-POLE of the story.

This is where the customer (the hero) appears to win and overcome opposition forces.

But a price is always paid for getting what you want.

Put another way: pride comes before a fall.

Which brings me to the third quarter and the fifth Story Code of *The Good the Bad and the Epic.*

The **Major Crisis**.

CHAPTER RECAP

CODE #4—PIVOT AT THE **MID-POINT**

The mid-point represents a dramatic shift in the direction of the narrative. Everything hinges on the mid-point.

Checklist:

☐ **Is your mid-point a false victory?** Introduce your solution at the midway mark, but not as a fait accompli. Your proposition still must be tested.

☐ **Have you kept the mid-point punchy?** Don't linger long at the mid-point. Move on quickly.

☐ **Have you ensured that the problem and the solution clash?** Make sure the solution at the mid-point addresses the customer's problem.

☐ **Have you built in an ordeal, death, and rebirth?** Is the story, and your customer, heading in a new positive direction thanks to your brand?

☐ **Do you build to a peak at the mid-point?** Build up your story to an anticipated reveal, or climax. Then, shift direction.

☐ **Have you made sure there is no going back?** This is the point of no return for your customer and your audience.

CHAPTER EIGHT

CODE #5—Hit a Major **Crisis**

*'If life was nothing but green lights and
we didn't have yellows and reds ...
hardships, crises, times for
introspection, then what the hell would
it all be for? We need the yellows and
the reds. That's how we evolve.'*

– Matthew McConaughey

A low point is a necessity of every great story.
Stories are more satisfying when a hero comes back from
the brink of defeat and succeeds. Trust and credibility are
earned only when a brand demonstrates that it can help a
customer overcome a major crisis.

MAKE YOUR LOWEST EBB YOUR FINEST HOUR

In February 2008, American instant film and camera company Polaroid filed for bankruptcy for the second time in seven years. They had limped through six CEOs and faced the same fate that would soon face Kodak.

Both were casualties of an unstoppable digital wave.

Polaroid was launched in 1937 by a scientist, Edwin H. Land, who developed the polarizer—a plastic sheet imbued with development chemicals. His invention enabled people to create a near-instantaneous image at the touch of a button.

Everyone, from Andy Warhol to the Rolling Stones (all epic storytellers), adored the Polaroid.

But, at the start of the millennium, digital cameras and smartphones began to decimate the camera industry.

Polaroid was in disarray.

In 2008, they announced a complete withdrawal from analogue instant film products.

But that's when a group of Dutch instant photography enthusiasts stepped in to save the day.

They bought the company and began producing instant film under the name *The Impossible Project*.

In an instant, Polaroid was resurrected.

In 2010 the company brought Lady Gaga in as a creative director and licensed several digital camera products.

In 2012, Polaroid and *The Impossible Project* united as allies to launch Polaroid Originals.

These were heritage-inspired cameras launched at a time when Millennials were looking for ways to bring originality to digital and 'old school' filters were surging.

They embraced the brand.

The Polaroid story is compelling because it incorporates our primal need for an **All is Lost** moment.

We're drawn to those who, at their lowest ebb, dig deep and find a new plan—a reason to believe again.

It's an idea that's as true for story marketing as it is for life. Overcoming setbacks. Never giving up.

Many iconic brands have returned from the brink of defeat—and made a story of triumph over adversity.

- Apple
- Lego
- Marvel
- Polaroid

What unites them is that, in each case, the brand was able to learn from mistakes and adapt to a changing world with an innovative new plan and fresh thinking.

They found methods to mimic disruptors and serve their customers in new ways without compromising their heritage. What makes them even more potent is that for every success story, there is a comparable failure story.

- Atari
- Blockbuster
- Debenhams
- Kodak

The list goes on.

We know that since 2000, over 50% of Fortune 500 companies have evaporated. The reason, according to most research analysts, is likely three-fold:

1. POST-SALE. Everything after the sale has a more significant value to us.

2. ON-DEMAND. We want access to experiences and products right away.

3. ATTENTION ECONOMY. If brands are unable to capture attention, they're lost.

Brands that don't find a way to navigate these three factors disappear. But brands that falter and *then* find a way will capture our imagination.

Why do these stories move us?

Because we relate to them on a personal level.

We crave the Major Crisis because it reminds us of the setbacks and defeats in our own lives and how we must all face them. It stems from the primal origin of all stories.

RAISE THE PRIMAL STAKES

Two hunters stand in the Kalahari Desert. It's a lonely place and full of threat: overwhelming heat, deadly scorpions, venomous yellow cobras, elephant, leopard, lion.

The men, having seen no sign of big game for a long while—and perhaps becoming inured to the wildness of the desert—leave their weapons in their Land Rover and walk across the hot sand to investigate some tracks.

Several prints. LARGE.

And recent.

As they approach, everything changes.

A roar snaps up their heads. Fifty meters from them, conjured by magic from the swirling dust of the desert, stands a massive black-maned beast in its prime.

A Kalahari lion.

The men glance back at their Land Rover. The situation is untenable. They'll never return to their vehicle's safety in time. Then, one of the men drops to his haunches and begins retying his shoelaces.

His friend looks at him in goggle-eyed amazement. '*Are you crazy?*' he says. '*You can't outrun a lion!*'

The first hunter, shoelaces tied, stands upright and wipes the sweat from his brow. '*I don't need to,*' he says grimly. '*All I have to do is outrun you.*'

It's an old joke, but it makes a good point.

When you hit rock bottom, you need a new plan that no one has seen coming. Put another way, primal jeopardy forces us to find innovative solutions.

In *Save the Cat*, Blake Snyder writes about the need for primal stories with 'stakes a caveman can understand'.

Primal is about Eating and Surviving—the prime factors in life. Everything else is stored under 'nice to have'.

Primal stories tap into our Stone Age Lizard Brains.

These are stories that reflect the foundational row of **Maslow's Hierarchy of Needs**.

Life and death. Survival. Protecting your home.

Will the hero survive?

How will they do it?

What reserves of courage and skill will they draw on?

Stories are more potent when the stakes are primal.

And you can easily apply this logic to marketing.

We know from behavioural psychology that loss aversion is a stronger motivator than gain, so demonstrate to your customers what's at stake—what they risk losing—if they *don't* choose your product or service.

Raise the PRIMAL STAKES.

CREATE A FALSE DEFEAT

Consider the following. A customer seeks to buy an SUV renowned for safety. She wants this new car because she's recently had a child. Her problem is therefore primal. She needs to keep her growing family safe.

Now, let's assume the average car ownership cycle for this SUV brand is four years. So, the mid-point of her brand relationship is at the two-year mark.

At this point, she's likely comfortable with her car, but nothing major has gone wrong.

In other words, she hasn't yet dealt with a major crisis:

- A service
- A repair
- A breakdown

She will feel loyal to the SUV brand *only* when the brand has handled a crisis and has safely got her back on the road.

A vehicle's customer lifecycle easily maps to *The Good the Bad and the Epic* circle and the essential role the Major Crisis plays in building a lasting bond with the brand.

Demonstrating how the brand responds positively in a crisis earns you customer trust—often for life.

However, life is seldom fair whereas marketing stories can *create* the narrative arc we crave.

So, when mapping out your customer lifecycle, introduce a major crisis two-thirds into their relationship with the brand. This allows you to plan for the worst possible scenario. And find innovative solutions.

In screenwriting, Blake Snyder suggests the page number of a well-structured script where this moment should arrive.

Page 75. Two-thirds into the story—where the old way of thinking must die, clearing a path for the new approach. It's an inverted moment that follows the mid-point of the story. However, in contrast to the False Victory of the mid-point, the Major Crisis is a **False *Defeat***.

We have what appears to be a victory for the *ant*agonist over the *prot*agonist. The forces of opposition have beaten out the goals of the customer (the hero).

But not for long.

The mid-point is not the story resolution.

Neither is the low point.

We're only two-thirds of the way through the story.

It's the comeback that will thrill us.

That's what we're waiting for—to see the hero digging deep and, ultimately, winning.

LOOK FOR THE GLITCH IN YOUR STORY

Stuart Butterfield is a famous Canadian entrepreneur and billionaire. He's one of the visionaries behind Flickr, the photograph-sharing website that was acquired by Yahoo! in 2005. Butterfield went on from that success to co-find a new gaming company called Tiny Speck in 2009.

The first multi-player game they launched was called:

Glitch.

Butterfield and his partners set to work creating tools to help build and expand on the game. But, unlike Flickr, it failed to capture a widespread fanbase. The game did earn a small following, but it wasn't enough.

They tried, and they failed to keep it alive.

Tiny Speck began winding *Glitch* down.

The game was up.

Glitch was Butterfield's darkest hour.

But the story doesn't end here.

In a eureka moment, Butterfield and his team realised the chat platform they had created to support game development was a product *any* team could use to be more productive. They'd invented a new business model.

The team chat company Slack was born in an All is Lost moment. In April 2019, Slack went public, and its shares rocketed to $21 billion. Not bad, Butterfield.

Defeats embolden us.

They force us to push harder, to go beyond.

To innovate.

And we ignore them at our peril.

In March 2015, I was a strategy consultant on a pitch for an account with the UK government's Trade and Investment Department (renamed the Department for International Trade). Their mission was to help overseas companies bring quality investment into the UK.

We set about the task with a clear and ambitious target.

Double the value of exports to £1 trillion by 2020.

Research told us that we needed to find successful exporters with a positive story to tell, thereby improving Britain's image as a viable investment opportunity.

The idea of building export advocacy and the multi-channel campaign that we developed to promote it seemed to fit the brief perfectly. The problem was that their budget wouldn't meet the campaign's needs.

In what became our defining mistake, we decided to deal with the budget issue later. The plan was simple.

Win the pitch, *then* address the budget.

We put together an excellent presentation—it was slick, and the creative ideas were blazing hot. On the day of the pitch, we were confident—and with good reason. The clients praised our strategic thinking and creativity.

We walked out of the pitch meeting thinking we had it in the bag. Then they came back with the bad news.

They loved our ideas—however, they decided to award the win to a competing agency with a similar idea. Though they admitted their campaign wasn't as refined as ours, what won the client over was that the other agency had told them the budget was undercooked.

It wasn't the biggest or best idea that won on the day.

It was a basic storytelling principle. We had dismissed the all-important role of the Major Crisis.

You *must* punch holes in your solution.

You *must* ask where the idea can falter.

We'd known that the budget was the glitch in the story. But instead of exposing the flaw, we chose to conceal it. A fatal error. *Not* telling the story of the low point lost us the pitch. A lesson I won't soon forget.

TURN YOUR FLAW INTO YOUR STRENGTH

David Beckham was vilified in England's 1998 World Cup football (soccer) match against Argentina. When he kicked Diego Simeone, Beckham was red-carded and sent off. Argentina won the game on penalties, and England was out.

Beckham bore the brunt.

He was treated as a pariah in his own country, even receiving death threats.

But Beckham earned his redemption four years later when he curled a free kick into the net against Greece, securing England a place in the next World Cup.

David Beckham's stubborn petulance earned him his red card in 1998. But this same stubbornness, redirected, drove his refusal to give up for four years, culminating in the match against Greece in 2002. England required a one-goal miracle in stoppage time to enter the World Cup.

Beckham stepped up and delivered.

A beautiful bending boot into the back of the net.

He went from being booed off the field to a national hero. Stubbornness was his flaw *and* his strength.

We're suckers for a story like this. A flawed hero rises from the ashes—back from the brink of defeat.

A reversal of fortune—a redemption.

It speaks to us on a mythological and personal level.

Richard Shotton, whose superb book *The Choice Factory* is essential reading for marketers, unpacks the idea further in an article for *Marketing Week*. He discusses a 1966 experiment by Harvard psychologist Elliot Aronson, who researched the benefit of exposing one's flaws.

Aronson recorded an actor answering a series of quiz questions. Armed with the correct responses, the actor answers 92% of the questions correctly. After the quiz, the actor pretends to spill a cup of coffee over himself. Aronson makes two recordings, one with the spill and one without. He then splits his students into two groups.

One group was shown the footage with the spill, the other without. Aronson then asked each group to assess the contestant's likability.

In every case, the students found the clumsy contestant significantly more likeable and relatable.

The takeaway?

We prefer people with a weakness.

It's an idea Aronson termed **The Pratfall Effect.**

This importance of likability—linked to our capacity to relate to the hero in a story—is reflected the title of Blake Snyder's book on screenwriting, *Save the Cat.*

The hero of a story must be likeable for the audience to be willing to follow them for the duration of the film. This is especially important if the protagonist is an antihero.

So, what does the screenwriter do?

They build in a moment—usually in the first five minutes of the film, at the introduction of the lead character—where the hero will do something that makes them likeable.

Hence Snyder's title.

They will 'save the cat' out of a tree.

It's a pivotal scene that defines the protagonist and makes us, the audience, relate to them.

We like the ostrich in the Samsung VR ad because of her independent spirit and willingness to make a fool out of herself in front of the flock.

We like Ava, the girl in John Lewis' *Excitable Edgar* ad, because of her kind attempts to keep Edgar's fire at bay.

And we like Edgar because of his clumsy enthusiasm.

An authentic character with faults, is far more interesting and more likeable than someone without flaws:

- Without his psychological scars, Batman is just a rich freak in a weird-looking bat suit.
- Superman without kryptonite is boring.
- The Mandalorian—and Clint Eastwood's 'man with no name' from the Sergio Leone westerns that inspired his creation (and the title of this book)—is compelling because of his skewed moral compass— he's an *antihero*, a dispassionate bounty hunter. He

kills people for a living, and yet he protects baby Yoda (or rather, Grogu).

The FLAW makes these characters fascinating (and holds the seed of their transformation). Most brands get this wrong all the time. They obsess about the perfection of their product. They create marketing communication that yells:

'LOOK AT ME!'

Epic brands take a different view.

Yes, they showcase their products in the very best light possible, but they're also honest about their shortcomings and failures. They present their products authentically, where the customers might see themselves reflected.

Remember, the brand isn't the hero of the story.

It's the customer.

Epic brands often don't just acknowledge their failures; they turn them into an *asset*.

Volkswagen's 1960 Beetle ad exemplifies this. Their *Think Small* campaign contrasted with the dominant view in the US at the time—which was all about thinking BIG.

VW turned that on its head and capitalised on their USP—the Beetle's small size and their quirky look.

A now famous ad, created by DDB, depicted the Beetle with a one-word heading:

Lemon.

The ad is powerful because of an underlying customer insight—*people are tired of big cars talking big talk.*

One of the ads even featured the clumsy-looking lunar landing module accompanied by a gem of a header:

It's ugly, but it gets you there.

Epic brands never shrink from exposing flaws.

Think of Guinness—*Good things come to those who wait.*

Or Stella Artois—*Reassuringly expensive.*

Epic brands make a story of their flaws.

Do the same for your brand. Be authentic.

This is a key part of effective marketing and it's intrinsic to *The Good the Bad and the Epic.*

Brand marketers must master the art of transforming a flaw into a strength.

Volkswagen—with their ad agency, DDB—didn't just create a great *Think Small* campaign, they changed the entire Advertising Industry. From that day forward a new approach opened. No more catchy jingles and slogans. Advertising became more honest. More intelligent. More human.

A recent example of a brand embracing their core weakness comes from Formula E. This all-electric motor racing series plays out in the streets of city centres around the world.

The problem is the sport wasn't turning a profit. Fans saw it as lacking emotion. To compete with the thrill of Formula One's combustion engines, something radical was required.

Together with their agency, Iris, the team realised that *electric* was both their problem *and* their solution.

Their strategy? Go from being seen as exciting *despite* being electric to being exciting *because* they were electric.

Inspired by video games, they introduced a 'power-up' zone that enabled drivers to gain a quick electric boost.

Its name? *Attack Mode.*

This game-changing innovation brought jeopardy and thrill into the sport, helping Formula E put sustainability on the map by winning new fans, and finally making a profit.

Formula E turned their flaw into their strength.

MAKE THE NIGHT DARKEST BEFORE THE DAWN

Michael Collins was the lesser-known member of the three-person Apollo 11 team sent to the moon.

Collins flew the Command Module.

After dropping off his famous colleagues, Buzz Aldrin and Neil Armstrong, he circled the moon for hours in darkness, cut off from the radio signal back to Earth.

In his words:

'*I am now truly alone. And absolutely alone from any known life. I am it.*'

For over 21 hours, he spun through the dark. As he watched the sun rise over the shoulder of the moon, Collins considered how the mission might not go as planned.

Eagle had never been fired on the moon. If it failed to take off, Collins would return to the Earth alone.

This image of Collins, floating beyond the moon, is a perfect way to imagine the story beat that happens after, and in direct response to, the All is Lost moment.

Blake Snyder calls it:

The Dark Night of the Soul.

We've all experienced it—hopelessness and despair.
The introspection that comes after a defeat.

- It's the lone ostrich in Samsung's ad, stretching out her wings in the moonlight

- It's Ava, the young girl in *Excitable Edgar*, sitting in midnight vigil outside his room

Stories are more poignant when a character has a crisis of confidence. But through perseverance and willpower, a moment arrives when the solution to the problem emerges.

A new dawn always follows the dark night of the soul.

Like the sun rising behind the moon for Michael Collins.

Chumbawamba echoes this beautifully with their one-hit-wonder song, *Tubthumping*:

> *'I get knocked down, but I get up again. You're never gonna keep me down.'*

It's a human idea—cause and effect.

Something knocks us down.

We get up again.

Drama *must* have this conflict.

Without it, we have no reason to follow a story—it moves forward on a flat path. No jeopardy. No threat to the status quo. The story is the journey. The trials we face, the false starts and the failures—the odyssey.

If you want to tell a brand story about how you solved a problem, don't go to the answer first. Show the wrong turns you took. The self-doubts. The miss-steps. The failures. Include a crisis moment—where you faltered and nearly gave up. But you didn't because you're made of sterner stuff.

When addressing customers, be truthful about their setbacks, pitfalls, and pain points.

Why?

Because nothing is won until all is lost. And the greatest lessons are learned in adversity.

****

No marketing story worth its salt is ever complete without failure or a major crisis. A crisis requires a new plan. The hero (the customer) and the brand (the mentor and guide) must face the problem and find a new path.

It's as true in life as it is in brand storytelling.

Don't gloss over failures or conceal them.

Revel in them.

It's only through a low point—a major crisis—that a hero looks inward and finds their resolve to win.

Every hero, at some point in their odyssey, wants to quit. To give up. They lose hope.

They tell themselves: 'I'm not equal to the task'.

But heroes somehow find strength within.

Something triggers them to believe in themselves again. It's the essence of the phrase: 'ride or die'.

That's the rallying cry of the hero to me.

A hero isn't passive.

They're all in.

They commit. They take an active role in dragging themselves out of the hole and damn the consequences.

Which brings me to the final quarter of *The Good the Bad and the Epic* and the sixth code.

Where we **defeat the villain**.

CHAPTER RECAP

CODE #5—HIT A MAJOR CRISIS

Show what's at stake if customers don't accept the brand into their lives. Show them what they stand to lose.

Checklist:

☐ **Have you turned your lowest ebb into your finest hour?** Have you identified or created a major crisis to demonstrate your brand's ability to respond?

☐ **Have you made your story stakes primal?** Have you acknowledged what's really at stake for the customer? What do they stand to lose?

☐ **Have you created a false defeat?** The mid-point solution must feel like it might not succeed.

☐ **Have you looked for the glitch in your marketing story?** Don't present the solution as a fait accompli. Punch holes in it. Test it to the limit.

☐ **Have you turned your flaw into your strength?** Epic brands never shrink from exposing flaws.

☐ **Have you made the night darkest before the dawn?** Have you reflected the moment when all hope is lost so you can pivot to the solution?

CHAPTER NINE

CODE #6—Defeat the **Villain**

'We stop checking for monsters under our bed when we realise that they're inside us.'

– Author Unknown

Opposites create conflict like sparks jumping across the terminals of a battery. Every hero needs a villain. This is the final obstacle that stands in the customer's way. The one thing holding them back from achieving their goal.

CREATE A FLOW FROM YIN TO YANG

If there was ever such a thing as a perfect line of copy, then Under Armour must have a strong contender.

The brand's 2015 *Rule Yourself* campaign set out to redefine what it means to be successful in training.

The finest of the ads for me is the Michael Phelps commercial because it underscores a potent storytelling principle—victory is always hard won.

It's the pain we endure that makes any success more rewarding and more meaningful.

We tell the story of the long, hard struggle because of what this endurance and willpower says about our character. Pain doesn't define character.

It reveals it.

This is where the true story lies.

Conflict—the battle we wage against the shadow self.

The Under Armour line uses antithesis to give it power.

It reflects the battle of will that lives in us all.

Seek it out on YouTube and be sure to watch the ad all the way through to its conclusion, because it's the final line of copy that is, in my opinion, perfect:

It's what you do in the dark that puts you in the light.

The line goes beyond selling a product to a place where we feel an affinity with the brand.

Under Armour knows that stories underpin everything we do in life.

The brand understands that the best way to connect with people is to empathise with the battles we all wage against our biggest villain—ourselves.

Under Armour owes a great deal to the marketing success of the Nike brand. Nike built a fanatical brand mythology on a powerful Jungian idea.

When the shadow voice inside you says: '*You can't,*' Nike says the opposite: '*You can.*'

Nike gives us call to action that awakens the hero within. *Just do it.*

Every day is a battle of willpower.

We battle our fears.

The naysayers.

Our own shadow. The voice inside that says: '*I'm too slow, too weak, too old. I'm not good enough.*'

We all have it. Two competing voices in our heads. The heckler and the hype man.

The one that says: '*Back away.*'

And the one that says: '*Jump!*'

The dark and the light.

Night and day.

Yin and yang.

Opposing forces drive energy through a story.

We find references to this in all cultures. From the Ancient Egyptians and the *Seven Hermetic Principles* to the Chinese philosophy of *Yin-Yang*.

Yin is the closed door and darkness.

Yang is brightness and light.

The yin-yang idea illuminates a notion of 'flow' between one state and another.

There is a relationship between the two states.

A balance.

They are two halves that complete a whole.

This relationship between opposites is the root of all storytelling, and it's critical to marketing.

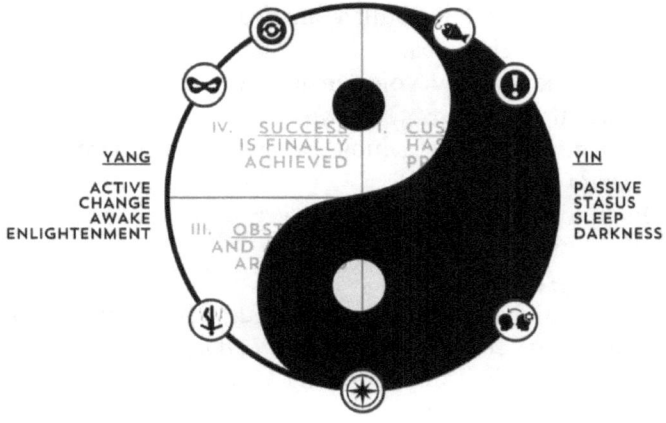

Figure 10: YIN-YANG AND THE SEVEN STORY CODES

All great stories are about transformation—an emotional or internal journey that the hero (the customer) must undergo.

It's a shift from limited awareness of their needs to an enlightened state of awareness.

At its most basic level, a story is an *Awakening*.

Therefore, mapping yin-yang to the story circle by plotting the dark half to the first hemisphere makes sense.

On the right, we have YIN.

On the left, YANG.

Before the mid-point, the hero has limited awareness of their problem and genuine need.

They might know what they *desire* but are stumbling around in the dark regarding their *need*.

They're going about things in the wrong way.

The role of the brand, as a mentor, is to guide them out of this darkness and into the light.

The brand brings them to the promised land by showing the customer a better version of themselves—so they can move to enlightenment. But only at the mid-point do they begin to see a ray of light, and only when they hit their lowest point—and confront their most profound hurt—will they find a new path.

You can apply this yin-yang narrative thinking to any customer journey.

The medical industry is a good example.

Take a patient journey—it begins with a problem.

Our patient (the hero) finds a lump, and they're rightfully concerned.

So, we have an *external* and an *internal* problem.

- External problem (desire): to rid themselves of the suspicious lump.
- Internal problem (need): to rid themselves of fear.

The physical villain in this story is 'the lump'.

That's the force of opposition the patient must face and overcome. But the true villain is FEAR—and there is no more primal emotion. Early humans faced a constant fear of being killed. So, we evolved a fight-or-flight mechanism.

The amygdala, a group of cells in the brain, gets triggered when we're in physical danger, causing a release of cortisol and adrenalin. The human body becomes 'hijacked' by the amygdala. All rational thought shuts down.

And we become instinctive.

Ready to run. Ready to fight.

Today, in the absence of these everyday primal threats, our amygdala is triggered by modern stress.

That's what the patient is feeling.

They're in the dark—afraid and unsure.

Fear leads to powerlessness and vulnerability.

It can also lead to resistance—a refusal to seek medical help (the refusal of the call).

At this point, the hero is still passive and in the dark. Nothing will change unless they act—they're in stasis.

Eventually, a family member of the patient (an ally) might convince them to see a doctor (the mentor).

And the long road to recovery can begin.

But it won't be a straight road.

The patient will have to commit to the diagnosis. It might involve trial and error—experimentation with different treatments. Things might go right for a while (at the mid-point), and then they might go wrong, and the patient might need surgery (the Major Crisis).

However, the patient is no longer passive.

They're taking an active role in their recovery.

They're shifting from the *yin* to the *yang*.

From the dark to the light.

FIND YOUR CUSTOMER'S DARTH VADER

Forces of opposition exist to make the hero's journey difficult. Their sole purpose is to create hardships and obstacles that test the hero and reveal their true character.

Brands must apply the same strategy.

Find the primary force of opposition that stands in the customer's path.

What represents the villain for the customer?

What prevents them from achieving what they need to accomplish?

Storytelling is a yearning that meets an obstacle.

Somebody wants something desperately.

And someone is hell-bent on stopping them.

Star Wars hinges on forces of opposition. When we first see Vader, he emerges like a shadow from a pall of smoke, all in black. He represents what Luke will become if he doesn't conquer his fear. Vader is Luke's shadow. Luke's conflict with the Dark Side is a battle with himself.

In great stories, the villain often reflects the hero's dark side. Confronting Vader is not just a physical conflict.

It's an emotional one.

It's about conquering the shadow—the voice of fear.

A strong protagonist MUST have a *stronger* antagonist pushing in the opposite direction.

A Voldemort for every Harry Potter.

A Joker for every Batman.

A Darth Vader for every Luke Skywalker.

Conflict becomes truly interesting when we understand that opposites blur into each other. Heroes and villains are reflections of each other. They are the light and the dark in us all. The hero *needs* the villain. And vice versa.

They give each other meaning.

Look at Ian Fleming's *Casino Royale*. James Bond is the hero. The book's villain is called le Chiffre. As with Vader and Luke, le Chiffre represents Bond's shadow. They are mirror images of each other. Think of it this way:

In French, le Chiffre means 'The Number'—a name that reflects a coldness of purpose—an unknowable, inhuman quality. And who is James Bond? On the surface, he's an ordinary man. We know his past—his Scottish father and his French mother. He's a human being, like us. But he's not.

With a licence to kill—he's an assassin.

James Bond is sympathetic with his charming persona façade, but he hides a flaw—a sociopathic alter ego.

And it's a number. OO7.

Le Chiffre.

OO7.

Both are cyphers—ruthless and implacable.

They compete for the same goal.

Le Chiffre is the shadow Bond carries with him—his darkness. Bond is effectively battling himself.

This idea that we all battle our shadow for the same goal is a central facet of *The Good the Bad and the Epic*.

Three ways to create a force of opposition:

1. **Find the tension in your customer insight.** Root out the natural tensions that exist in your target audience. Teens, for example, are desperate to avoid alienation *but* also seek to assert their individuality. Tensions lead to epic insights and communication.

2. **Present a plan to help the customer overcome the opposition.** The brand's role is to present a strategy to defeat the villain (the customer's shadow self, or an opposing brand delivering a poor-quality service). Steve Jobs famously set up forces of opposition when he introduced the iPhone. He talked about the problem all other existing smartphone brands (the opposition) presented—the *qwerty* keyboard that took up so much space on the interface. Introducing opposition failures allowed Steve Jobs to showcase the iPhone as the ultimate answer to the problem— making it immediately desirable.

3. **Ensure you've considered ALL barriers to your solutions.** Villains always have minions that assist them in making life difficult for the hero. The more pressure applied, the more the hero is forced to act. In marketing, this means you must consider *all* barriers that might stand in the path of your solution. Typically, these relate to four factors: People, Process, Technology, and Culture. Dove's *Real Beauty* positioning, which advocates women should define their own beauty standards, has catapulted sales in the West. US sales for Dove jumped from $2.5 to $4 billion in the campaign's first ten years, 2004-2014. However, the idea failed to resonate in developing countries. Why? Because they ignored the role of external admiration in markets outside of the West. Dove overlooked the cultural barriers.

A villain, or force of opposition, is potent when it reflects existing divisions—in culture and in ourselves. But often a villain in a well-crafted story is an entity or a concept.

In *Gravity*, the villain is SPACE—manifested as a debris cloud hurtling around the Earth.

In *Ostrich*, Samsung's VR headset commercial, the villain is CONFORMITY—the pull of the herd.

It reflects the brand's rivalry with Apple.

In Nolan's *Interstellar*, the film's opposition force and true villain is best articulated by Michael Caine's character (the mentor), delivering this gem of a line:

'I'm not afraid of death. No, I'm an old physicist. I'm afraid of time.'

Interstellar, Tenet, and *Memento.* The villain in each of these films is TIME. Even The Dark Knight Trilogy portrays TIME as the ultimate villain.

Batman is mortal.

Time is the only nemesis he can't conquer.

Have you identified the villain in *your* brand story?

Who represents the primary force of opposition?

BUILD A RIVALRY

'Imagine it is the evening of October 14th, 1988. Imagine you are Christopher White driving home. You're extremely tired and not watching the road properly.'

So begins a 1990 TV commercial made in South Africa. It tells the mind-blowing story of a businessman who lost control of his Mercedes-Benz while driving home along Chapman's Peak, a twisting road on a steep mountainside.

White blasted through roadside barriers and plunged down a cliff the equivalent of a thirty-storey building.

Miraculously, he survived with hardly a scratch.

The commercial voiceover closed as follows:

'Christopher White survived this 100-meter plunge for two reasons. He was wearing his seatbelt. And he was driving a Mercedes-Benz'.

The tagline?

Engineered like no other car in the world.

Fantastic stuff!

A campaign that won the brand many accolades and fans.

But then came an epic twist.

BMW, their premier rival, stepped in with a fiendishly clever response. They released their own Chapman's Peak commercial. It featured a BMW 5 series navigating the same tight curves and bends of this notorious Cape Town road. But at the exact place where the Mercedes-Benz went off the road, the BMW swerves, then corners perfectly.

And we hear the voiceover deliver this:

'Doesn't it make sense to drive a luxury sedan that beats the bends?'

A beautiful play on words.

Bends ... Benz.

BMW only ran the ad over a single weekend—they were concerned there might be a legal response.

There was, but the ad became a talking point for years to come, earning both brands airtime, new customers, and loyal fans. A rivalry that led to runaway success.

Competitive advertising is now banned in South Africa, but we still see the rivalry play out in Europe. In 2019, when Mercedes-Benz CEO Dieter Zetsche decided to call it a day, BMW was there with what seemed like a touching tribute.

In the ad, called *The Last Day*, we see a lookalike Zetsche bidding his staff farewell, making his way out of Daimler headquarters. He's driven home in a Mercedes-Benz sedan, looking wistfully out the window.

His driver shakes his hand and leaves him standing in the driveway.

We cut to a line of copy:

Free at last.

The garage door slides open.

We see the nose of a vintage Mercedes-Benz ...

Then, the twist.

A gold BMW i8 Roadster rips through the garage doors and, grinning at the wheel, Zetsche. He drives away in joy.

Thank you, Dieter Zetsche, reads the line of copy on the screen, *for so many years of inspiring competition.*

Boom! Mic drop.

Who doesn't love a great rivalry?

But, given we've established the customer is the hero and not the brand, what does a brand's rivalry with another brand matter to the customer?

Well, it's tribal—*us* v. *them.*

- BMW v. Mercedes-Benz
- Pepsi v. Coca-Cola
- Adidas v. Puma
- McDonald's v. Burger King
- Apple v. Microsoft

Have you ever wondered why Apple hands out those logo stickers in their product boxes?

They're to cover up any Windows gear logo.

Essentially, to hide your shame.

Rivalries are rife in brand marketing—as in sport and life. We invest in one side or another in the rivalry because of what it says about ourselves.

Do we want to be seen as more like Federer—graceful and serene under pressure, or more like Nadal, tenacious, muscular, and indomitable, like a bull?

These two opposing titans brought out the best in tennis. Think about that famous photograph of Federer and Nadal, both in tears when Roger retired from professional tennis.

We loved their rivalry because it fuelled the game.

But the picture brings home that they loved their rivalry just as much. It brought out the best in them and it gave us a compelling story to follow.

Look at a sport like football (soccer in the US).

In the United Kingdom, a derby game—like Manchester United v. Liverpool or Chelsea v. Manchester City—draws fanatical support from both sides. Visiting fans must often be bussed away under police guard.

Making an opposing team 'the villain' brings out primal emotions. In marketing, the villain is the rival brand.

Apple created an award-winning, longstanding campaign in 2006 that hit this idea on the nose.

I'm a Mac.

Apple struck gold by personifying the products:

- **Mac** was portrayed as the creative dude in a casual pullover and jeans (i.e. Steve Jobs)

- **PC** was depicted as the conservative business guy in a stiff suit (i.e. Bill Gates)

By positioning PC users as boring non-creatives, Apple was able to create space between the brands.

And that's how you create a cult following.

It might not seem rational.

But *Rational* doesn't persuade people to act.

Emotion does.

Three ways to build a rivalry:

1. **Seek out your primary opponent**. This is the brand with similar products and services (potentially better than yours, since the best villains are always more powerful than the protagonist). Most importantly, your primary opponent will be the brand competing for the same goal—*your* target audience.

2. **Widen the gap through ideology**. Make your main opponent the villain. Create values that reflect your target audience but oppose the values of your rival brand, as Apple did with Mac v. PC.

3. **Be cheeky but not aggressive about the rivalry**. Use pathos and humour, the same way BMW did with Mercedes-Benz. However, be sure to point out competitor brand failures the way Steve Jobs was able to do when he outlined the shortcomings of every single one of the brands that Apple is competing against in the smartphone market. In one fell swoop, he rendered them all far behind the curve.

One of my favourite examples of the effectiveness of creating a rivalry comes from a 2014 article in the Harvard Business Review. ePrize CEO Josh Linkner led a company with double- and triple-digit growth but was concerned that creativity might decline as they became the market leader. He was worried that they would start clinging to their previous success instead of forging new success.

Linkner realised they didn't have a competitor to gun against. So, what did he do?

He invented a rivalry.

Linkner made up a fake start-up nemesis called Slither. He even reinforced a message of their innovation and competitiveness with fake press releases.

The result?

The story began to drive increased performance.

And whiteboards overflowed with creative ideas.

Linkner understood the power of rivalry to motivate his team to work harder and to drive innovation.

But here's a stark warning—don't get so caught up in existing rivalry (real or fake) that you lose sight of a new entrant. The following longstanding, well-known rivalry— or rather, feud—will demonstrate this point.

A feud that ignited in 1975 with *The Cold Wars*.

Pepsi v. Coca-Cola.

Coca-Cola was the dominant brand in the early twentieth century. They even had a role in shaping Father Christmas. Their 1931 campaign depicted a wholesome, jolly Santa in a red outfit for the first time. Before that, he was in a green outfit. But in '75, rival Pepsi launched a stroke of marketing genius—*The Pepsi Challenge*.

It proved through a blind taste test that more people prefer Pepsi over Coke. A sweet success.

Pepsi began corroding Coca-Cola's market share, leading to this fiasco: Coca-Cola's switch-up to *New Coke* in 1985.

And we all know how that went down.

It's still seen as one of the all-time marketing missteps.

Coca-Cola was hit with a massive backlash from angry consumers, forcing them to return, in just three months, to their original formula—rebranded Coca-Cola Classic.

For years, Coca-Cola and Pepsi have been at each other's throats. The problem is that they became so embroiled in their own fizzing feud—trying to outwit and outmanoeuvre each other—that they didn't see the real opposition rising.

Today, neither brand is the bestselling energy drink.

In their early consumer testing, Red Bull received an overwhelmingly negative response. People hated the taste! But that didn't dent sales, because customers loved the brand ethos. Red Bull turned their industry upside down by positioning Coca-Cola and Pepsi as a united villain.

They were the old guard—stale and out of touch.

Red Bull positioned itself as more than just a drink (they hardly mention the word 'drink' in their communications).

Instead, they associate with the word 'energy'.

They fly in the face of a smiling Santa brand and align with an antithetical worldview.

Extreme sports.

Adrenalin.

Adventure.

Red Bull doesn't mind that the drink tastes awful.

They've turned that flaw into a strength!

But epic brands like Coca-Cola never get left behind.

Despite having one of the most recognisable logos in the world, they've embraced a polymorphic idea. In other words, they shapeshift to put the customer first. In 2011 they replaced Coca-Cola from one side of their bottles with the phrase *Share a Coke* followed by a person's name. Now that's making your customer the hero. And instead of being too precious about their logo, they went further in 2024, with *Every Coca-Cola is Welcome*, when they embraced and showcased interpretations of their logo from bodegas, shopkeepers and local artists from around the world.

To compete with rivals, Coca-Cola transcends language and culture and remains fresh in our minds by innovating what it stands for without corroding its heritage.

Opposing forces lead to conflict, intensity, and emotion.

There are so many examples in marketing.

One even prompted a 2019 film about the 1966 Le Mans race. The title? Ford v. Ferrari.

Adidas and Puma even set two brothers against each other in a bitter personal battle.

The higher the stakes and the emotional intensity of the conflict, the higher the audience engagement.

Creating a rivalry also drives innovation.

Take the Multiplex industry. The UK's most lucrative cinema chain today (at publication) is Vue.

Vue was able to leapfrog rivals, Odeon and Cineworld by studying and exploiting their shortcomings.

How?

Through AI innovation.

Instead of sticking to the industry standard schedules of their competitors, Vue introduced AI to monitor the habits of its customers so it can tailor schedules to better suit their needs. Vue cinemas in the UK all follow different schedules every day based on an algorithm that forecasts admissions and predicts everything from popcorn to seating choice.

Now that's a blockbuster idea.

An idea that sprang from Vue's strategy of studying its rivals and pivoting in a new, more innovative direction.

Brands win when they escalate forces of opposition.

They win when they create a **rivalry**.

LEAVE VICTORY TO THE VERY END

All great stories must build inexorably towards the final battle and the resolution—the catharsis your audience craves. Don't let them down.

The final quarter of *The Good the Bad and the Epic* is when we wrap things up and dispatch the 'bad guy'.

In Samsung's *Ostrich* ad, the Bad Guy is *conformity*.

At first, our hero ostrich tries to beat the opponent (and fly) the wrong way. She makes a public spectacle of herself right in the middle of the flock, trying to win their attention. She does. But in the opposite way to what she intended.

She earns derision—not adulation.

Only after the mid-point, when she removes herself from the flock and goes through a major crisis of confidence, can she find a new path to success. She no longer needs the approval of the flock. Having finally beaten the opposing forces, she can now take to the sky. In the final scene, we see the flock chasing after *her*. She has become a leader, not a follower. And the world order is forever changed.

This is the catharsis that every brand marketer must deliver in their communications. It's a final resolution where the hero defeats the villain. And you *must* tie it to your theme. That's the heart of the story you're telling.

In this case: *Do what you can't.*

Samsung is saying:

'Don't follow the flock. Break free.'

What Samsung managed with this commercial was to capture and *hold* our attention for the duration of the ad.

How did they do this?

By telling a story that has all the emotional beats and that leads us to a natural and compelling conclusion. They know a great story is only complete once the monster is tamed.

We cheer for the retribution John Wick, Jack Reacher, and The Bride in *Kill Bill* rain down. Because they resolve the injustice of an unfair world.

In real life, the guy who steals your car gets away with the crime, and the police never catch him.

But in fiction—as in marketing—we have the ability give audiences the ending they desperately crave.

We can defeat the villain.

And *that* story—of overcoming the opposition—is catnip to an audience enthralled by the unfolding drama.

As a marketer, you have the power to move people.

Your goal is to build towards the catharsis we crave.

The Resolution.

****

Stories need villains because villains make the hero rise.

Starbucks needs Dunkin Donuts.

PlayStation needs Xbox.

Dove's Real Beauty campaign needs the media villain of industry-imposed beauty ideals.

Villains force heroes to dig deep and overcome.

That's their role—to heap pressure on the hero.

Why?

Because character is revealed under pressure. Setting up a force of opposition is fundamental to a great story. Without the pressure the villain applies, the hero will never learn anything and change. Opposing forces brings about change through conflict. So, draw your lines in the sand.

Separate yin from yang.

Because *that*'s the heart of your brand story.

Conflict.

Opposing forces are a key component of *The Good the Bad and the Epic*. Don't smooth over them. Fuel them.

Make your customers fans. And then, when you get to the end everyone expected and wanted, subvert.

Close with a twist.

CHAPTER RECAP

CODE #6—DEFEAT THE VILLAIN

Every story must have a hero and a villain or main opponent. Forces of opposition make life difficult for the hero. Battling and overcoming them offers the resolution we crave.

Checklist:

☐ **Have you created a flow from yin to yang?** Have you established how to move your customer from their problem state (darkness) to the promised land (enlightenment)?

☐ **Have you found your customer's Darth Vader?** Find your customer's chief enemy. This will be the most potent force of resistance that stands in their way—and often, it's themselves.

☐ **Have you created a rivalry?** Tribes are created when we acknowledge a rivalry, usually with a powerful opponent seeking the same goal. Use this opposition. Build and fuel a mentality of *us v. them*.

☐ **Have you left victory to the very end?** Stories must build to the resolution in a satisfying way. Build anticipation. Defeat the villain last.

CHAPTER TEN

CODE #7—Close with a **Twist**

*'Finally reaching the tower where the
princess is being kept, the hero finds
she's not there ... it's a trap!'*

– Blake Snyder

The final image of a marketing story offers a resolution to
the customer's problem. The point is to show how the
brand journey transforms the customer. But the best brand
stories always leave us wanting more.

DELIVER THE DÉNOUEMENT

Is there such a thing as a perfect end to a story? I think so. Although, humans have a predilection for being proved wrong at the end of a story. We *want* the rug ripped out from under our feet—just as Keyser Söze did when, in the final moments of *The Usual Suspects*, Verbal, hobbled away from his police interview, and his limp gave way to a stride.

We were duped. And we *loved* it.

- A timid narrator turns out to be the villain
- A hero with miracle fighting skills was blind
- The lead character was dead the whole time

Stories that close with a twist-in-the-tail live long after the final scene. They prompt endless debate and discussion. And the good ones are unforgettable:

- *The Usual Suspects*
- *The Book of Eli*
- *The Sixth Sense*

Mark Kermode, author of *The Sense of an Ending: Studies in the Theory of Fiction,* says we want stories to:
'*Upset the ordinary balance of our naïve expectations*'.

In simple terms, nothing is better than saying:
'*I did not see that coming.*'

Blake Snyder calls it **The Hightower Surprise**.

In a marketing context, a Hightower Surprise—or ending with a plot twist—is equally effective as it is in Film.

One that never fails to move me comes from a pair of Film students who created a spec ad for Johnnie Walker.

Dear Brother opens with two men walking side-by-side down a deserted road in the dramatic wilderness of the Isle of Skye in Scotland. At the mid-point (45 seconds into the 90 second commercial), they rest in the wreck of a burnt-out building and share a glass of Johnnie Walker Black.

Then continue down the road, until they arrive at a cliff.

A spoken word poem delivers a moving soundtrack:

'Cool my demons and walk with me, brother.
Until our roads lead us away from each other ...'

The camera pans around them, and we see the twist.

One of the men disappears.

The remaining man tips an urn to the wind, and we watch the ashes float away. He was a ghost.

It's a heart-breaking ad that showcases the talents of the directors and exemplifies the power of a twist ending.

In Chapter Seven, I introduced *Excitable Edgar*, the green dragon character, in the John Lewis and Waitrose Christmas commercial. I said I wouldn't give the ending away ... until now that is. We begin with Ava and Edgar walking through a snowy village. Edgar tries and fails to join the Christmas fun of building snowmen and ice skating. But fire-breathers and snow make terrible bed mates. Chaos ensues.

At the mid-point, when Ava looks to have the situation beaten, Edgar burns down the town tree.

Now we hit the Major Crisis. Edgar is in hiding. Ava can't coax him out until she gets an idea.

And here comes the twist.

Ava and Edgar arrive at the town's Christmas dinner. Imagining fireballs, everyone ducks for cover. Like us, they expect the worst. But Edgar hauls out a rum-soaked pudding and, with a gentle snort, sets it to flame. Christmas wins.

It's a clever resolution but, for me, you'll find the best twist ending in a John Lewis ad in *The Long Wait*.

A boy counts down the days to Christmas. Like any child, we assume and *expect* that he's anxious to unwrap his own presents. He watches the clock, willing the hands to accelerate. At the mid-point, as if by magic, snow arrives.

Then, at the close of the commercial, the boy wakes on Christmas morning, leaps out of bed, fetches a gift from the tree, bursts into his parents' room, and delivers *his* gift to *them*. A beautiful twist that plays with our bias.

Volvo manage to capture our attention and our hearts with a dynamic storytelling approach to their marketing. In 2024 they broke all the snackable social media rules with a 3-minute, 46-second Instagram ad shot by Hoyte van Hoytema, the visionary cinematographer and storyteller behind *Interstellar* and *Oppenheimer*. The ad was especially impactful and provocative because it came hot on the heels of Jaguar's rebranding spectacle just days earlier.

But Volvo's story-led ad isn't a new approach for the brand. The clever twist it lands at the end of the ad echoes a commercial the brand released seven years earlier.

Volvo *Moments* is a three-minute commercial that begins with a girl who is apprehensive about her first day of school. The girl's mother tells her to imagine that she's in control.

So begins an imagined future. We see her making new friends. Travelling the world. Experiencing life's wonders, including an awakening ritual, or rebirth, at the mid-point.

Thereafter, it's about falling in love, breakups and pain, and an unfulfilled job—the Major Crisis. Then, a new plan: a more creative, passionate career, a family, a home.

As the story concludes, we cut back to reality—a Volvo on a collision course with the girl as she crosses a road.

But here's the twist.

It's not the shocking accident the ad primed us for. Instead, the vehicle stops in time thanks to Volvo's safety technology. The closing copy line says it all:

Sometimes the moments that never happen matter the most.

Every great story must deliver a dénouement (a French word meaning *untie the knot*). All the complex story threads you've woven need to be *untangled* in the end for the audience. But don't sew things up too neatly. Twist the end.

REMEMBER THE PEAK-END RULE

A colonoscopy is an unusual place to find a discovery about memory, but Psychologist Daniel Kahneman managed it all the same. At the time of his research—1993—a colonoscopy was painful and there was variability. Sometimes it would hurt a great deal. Other times, it was just unpleasant.

Plus, the time it took would vary.

Kahneman asked his patients to rate the pain from 0 to 10 throughout the procedure.

Post-procedure, he asked patients for their evaluations of the procedure's total pain and related these to the real-time recording during the experience.

Kahneman learned we remember an experience based on its **peak** moment (pleasant or unpleasant) and its **ending**.

But *not* on how long the experience lasted.

Kahneman realised we have two selves:

1. The Remembering Self
2. The Experiencing Self

The Remembering Self makes our decisions based on how we perceive the past, but it doesn't always do what's best for the Experiencing Self.
Why?
Because our memories are subject to bias.
And peaks of emotion.

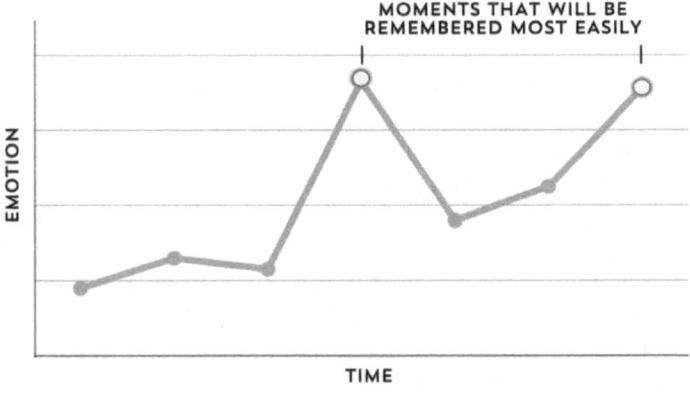

Figure 11: THE PEAK-END RULE

The **Peak-End Rule** defines the way we summarise any experience—and how we use this to remember how the experience felt and whether we'll go through it again. What does this mean for marketing? It means there are two critical parts of your story for better retention value:

1. **The highlight moment**: where you have a strong peak of emotion (negative or positive)

2. **And the last moment**: where everything is resolved (and left a little open, too)

Two ways to apply the Peak-End rule:

1. **Deliver a moment of intense emotion.** Messages that make people feel *strong* emotions (positive or negative) are proven to be more effective than communications that are, on average, expressive but don't deliver any extreme highs or lows. Deliver an intense story climax through humour, heartbreak, or shock. Reach this peak of emotion at the mid-point.

2. **Make the end a tease.** We base our brand choices on our last best experience. If the story conclusion is epic, our retention increases. That's why a twist-in-the-tail works so effectively in marketing stories. The end must tease the audience and leave them wanting more.

START AT THE END

A great story will take us on a journey into the heart of darkness and *back*. The return is critical. The hero must face their fears and finally overcome them.

For example:

- If they cannot 'let go' at the start, they must become capable of 'letting go'
- If they're hopeless at the start, they must be full of hope at the end
- If they're self-centred at the beginning, they must become selfless at the end

The writer's job is to show the transformation the hero has undergone. A way to do this is to have the opening and closing images reflect each other.

That's why the **Seven Code Framework** is a circle—to show what the hero has learned through their experiences.

As an example from cinema, compare the opening and closing images of the film *Raging Bull:*

- **Opening image**: Jake LaMotta is a muscular athlete shadowboxing in a boxing ring (his crucible). The scene is DREAM-LIKE.

- **Closing image**: LaMotta is an overweight has-been still shadowboxing. He is seen in a shabby bathroom mirror, a brutal reflection of his REALITY.

Raging Bull is a tragedy because it charts the story of a man who cannot beat his demons. At the close of the film, we find LaMotta well past his prime, but still shadowboxing.

This link between opening and closing images applies to all great marketing. Consider for example the commercials I've referred to most often in the book:

- Samsung – *Ostrich*
- John Lewis & Waitrose – *Excitable Edgar*

SAMSUNG – *Ostrich*

- **Opening image**: We're looking DOWN from the sky on a flock of ostriches, indistinguishable from each other in the dry dust of the desert.

- **Closing image**: We're looking UP from the desert and the rippling shadow of a single ostrich flying into the blue and limitless sky.

JOHN LEWIS & WAITROSE – *Excitable Edgar*

- **Opening image**. We see Ava and Edgar OUTSIDE, walking through a cold, snow-bound village, isolated from the rest of the townspeople.

- **Closing image**. We see Ava and Edgar INSIDE, standing in front of the entire village, cheered on and welcomed as one of the townspeople.

Opening and closing images are stark reminders of the core role of any story—to chart a transformation.

They hold the essence of the story arc. But, as any writer will tell you, the beginning of a story is hard to find.

Authors will constantly rewrite the opening lines, looking for a way to encapsulate the hero's state *before*.

Edgar Allen Poe advocates a different approach:

'*Go to the end of the story first.*'

- How will the main character evolve?
- How will they win in the end?
- What better, richer state will the hero achieve?

Poe would define the end state first, then return to the beginning to build a contrasting image—the absolute opposite state he could imagine. *That* became the start.

The best way to build a skeleton spine of your marketing story is often the same way—in *reverse.*

Find the opposite state to the end of your narrative, and it might spark a brilliant idea about how to begin.

It's a technique you can apply to any brand marketing message, or a news article. Click on a lead story on any magazine site, and you'll see how the end of the article resolves the beginning and how the writer ties the last paragraph to the first. A writer must ensure a chapter's start and end open and close on a linked idea.

This is as true for a *paragraph* as it is for *a chapter* or an entire *novel*. In the same way, screenwriters will ensure that all *scenes* and *Acts* have circular patterns.

The start of a scene poses a question that only the end of the scene will resolve (or at least push the story forward by opening a new, related question).

Marketers acutely aware of this can deliver the resolution we all crave—but with a twist.

It's the ending we want but not how we expect.

EARN THE RESOLUTION

An epic twist-in-the-tail isn't a mandate, but earning the resolution *is* required. You can't drop it into the story out of the blue. There's a name for that sort of conceit:

Deus ex Machina (God from the Machine).

This is when something is introduced abruptly into the story, providing a contrived solution to the problem.

The hero is about to be killed by the dragon when he stumbles over a magic sword he uses to slay the monster.

No good.

The storyteller must set up—and *earn*—the final scene and experience.

This is equally true for a brand story.

1. **DEFINE your vision**. Be clear about your purpose. Simon Sinek says: 'Don't *start with WHAT, start with WHY*.' Why do you exist in the world? Nike doesn't sell shoes. It sells the idea that anyone can be an athlete.

2. **PROMOTE your vision**. Set expectations. Make a pledge to your audience. Be clear about how you intend to resolve the customer's problem. Be sure your promise and proposition differ from all the competitor players already in the market.

3. **DELIVER your vision in an unexpected way**. Be disruptive. Bring a new customer experience no one imagined possible. With the iPhone launch, we expected an innovative new phone to compete with the many keyboard smartphones of the time, but no one imagined a phone with a screen that we could swipe our fingers across. No one ever imagined a car with four wheels when they expected a faster horse. No brand considered delivering a premium espresso experience to our homes. Until ...

At the push of a button, you can experience a smooth Italian-blend espresso in the comfort of your home—this is the promise Nespresso pledges. Their model?

A machine-and-pod coffee concept for making quality espresso at home bought from sophisticated boutiques to get that elite community coffee vibe and make their customers feel part of a movement. And the model works.

At publication, the Nespresso brand has 10 million online subscribers and more than 800 brightly lit boutiques in around 84 countries and their revenues are in the billions.

This is significant because their machines aren't cheap, and their coffee pods are more expensive than buying a bag of beans. So, why is the brand so successful?

Because Nespresso don't just talk about their vision.

They deliver it.

- Their brand ambassador, George Clooney, gives them a sophisticated appeal
- Their boutique stores ooze membership
- Their sleek coffee machines are modern-looking and effortless to use
- Their aluminium pods are jewel-coloured
- Their coffee taste is smooth and earns the cost

From machine purchase, to buying the pods, all the way to taking that first sip at home, Nespresso delivers its vision at every step of the customer journey, end-to-end.

Like any marketing story, the resolution—that first sip of the elixir at the culmination of the journey—is *earned.*

Every story must end like a well-crafted joke.

On a punchline. And, to earn that punchline, you must set it up long before it's delivered.

Story-led brands are successful because they operate with a clear end goal in mind: to transform the lives of their customers. In doing so, they transform themselves:

- **From rational to emotional**. Brands that create and deliver appeal through emotion, not facts, make customers remember them more readily.

- **From business-first to customer-first**. Brands that solve customer problems are admired more those that impose a business will on their customers.

- **From transaction-driven to relationship-driven**. Story-led brands prioritise long-term brand loyalty and engagement over short-term gains.

- **From product-led to purpose-led**. Storytelling brands have an end goal that reaches beyond the product to earn a more meaningful vision.

GIVE THEM A LEAVE

Aaron Sorkin, author of *A Few Good Men* and *The West Wing*, says you must give your audience a Leave. It's an idea from the game of Pool, where a player won't just be thinking about the current shot they're playing, but where they want to *leave* the cue ball for the next shot. And the shot after that.

Epic storytelling is all about the Leave.

A question answered that prompts a new question.

Any one of the great series on Amazon Prime, Netflix, Disney+, HBO and many more reflect this. Binge-worthy shows compete for and win our attention *and* engagement.

Think of *Succession* or *The Crown*.

They understand how to keep our interest.

How?

They follow the beats of narrative structure.

They know that only through this invisible story method can audience interest be reliably created and *maintained*.

Look at all the episodes of *The Queen's Gambit* which was streamed on Netflix.

It's not hard to see the Seven Story Codes reflected. The season maps so cleanly to them it's almost uncanny. But this is not some prescient force at play—it's the universal Monomyth in action. And the power of narrative structure:

1. **Openings**
2. Exchanges
3. Doubled pawns
4. **Middle game**
5. Fork
6. Adjournment
7. **End game**

Each episode tells a contained story that ends in a way designed to make us hunger for what will follow.

Each season also has a narrative arc to complete. A story that moves from a hook to a mid-point to a resolution or Leave in the final scene of the final episode.

Marketing can and *must* learn from all these storytelling beats. Modern marketers, like filmmakers, know that a Leave is a powerful way to garner engagement and go viral. That's why epic endings are often ambiguous.

They leave audiences wanting answers.

They compel us to think.

They prompt a debate in social media.

Remember, we *want* to work for our meal.

That's half the fun of an ambiguous ending. It forces us to make up our own minds about the story's outcome. And then discuss. But audiences still crave the resolution. An end that's too ambiguous can feel like the author didn't know how to close the story. Conversely, too sown up can feel trite. The key is to find the balance.

My advice?

Leave them on a cliffhanger.

It's the Zeigarnik Effect all over again (see **CODE #1: Open with a Hook**). Audiences need to know what happens next when the end is left open.

I call it **Perfect Imperfection**.

In the final moments of the third and last film in Nolan's Batman trilogy, *The Dark Knight Rises*, we see Batman fly out over the bay into the sun, carrying a ticking bomb that he, like all of us, cannot escape.

TIME.

Then, there follows a famous twist in the tale.

Years later, Alfred sees Bruce Wayne alive and well on a restaurant terrace in Rome. But *is* he seeing him?

Or is this Alfred's wishful thinking?

The ambiguity is compelling.

It's left open for debate.

You want the ending to agitate your audience.

To get them talking.

So, build a conclusion that's inevitable *and* surprising.

A perfect imperfect end.

CHAPTER RECAP

CODE #7—CLOSE WITH A **TWIST**

A story ending must be satisfactory for the audience. We want a resolution. But *also,* something unexpected.

Checklist:

- ☐ **Have you delivered a dénouement?** We need the resolution the story has set up. But nothing gets us talking more than a surprise twist in the tail.

- ☐ **Have you remembered the Peak-end Rule?** A story with peaks and troughs of emotion is better than one that flatlines. Experiences are remembered for their most intensely emotional moment and the impact of the last moment.

- ☐ **Have you started at the end?** For any story to work, you must have a destination in mind, because if you don't know where you're going there's a good chance you won't get there. So, consider where you want to leave the audience and work backwards to the beginning.

- ☐ **Have you earned your brand story resolution?** Making a promise to your audience and keeping it with a resolution is key to great marketing.

- ☐ **Have you given the audience a leave**? Epic stories agitate us. They leave us wanting mor

CHAPTER ELEVEN

Putting it into Practice

*'Budweiser loves to tell stories—whole
movies, really, crunched into 30
seconds. And people love them.'*

– Keith Quesenberry

Jeff Bezos believes in the power of storytelling so much that
he banned slide presentations from his board meetings.
Instead, Bezos (when he was still CEO of Amazon)
demanded that his executives submit a six-page idea
memo. Writing the memos forced his team to think more
deeply about their ideas and create a more persuasive
structure for them. The Bezos Memo is a potent reminder
that getting your message across requires critical thinking
and the ability to build an argument with story.

And it works no matter the marketing format.

Look at the study on the halftime Superbowl ads by Johns
Hopkins University.

Keith Quesenberry conducted a two-year analysis of 108
Superbowl commercials.

Quesenberry found that people prefer ads that tell a
story—in other words the commercials that follow clear
narrative beats. But don't take Quesenberry's word on this

(or mine). Watch the 2015 Budweiser *Lost Dog* Commercial on YouTube and you'll see what I mean. Sure, this is expensive advertising, but it's the *story* that grabs us.

And *all* the story codes are here:

- The hero with a problem: the puppy, far from home
- The mid-point: where we see the farm again
- The Major Crisis: the wolf

And so on. It's Odysseus again. The epic return.

Now you might be thinking, given my references so far, that storytelling technique applies only to B2C brands.

It doesn't.

Storytelling campaigns have delivered some incredible successes for iconic B2B brands, like: Adobe, Cisco, HP. And, more recently: Pinterest, Slack and Squarespace.

BLP, a law firm offering advice to financial institutions, generated 515% more leads than their target with a YouTube campaign featuring cautionary tales about bankers that fail to follow regulatory advice (according to b2bmarketing.net).

With a B2B offering you're not persuading a *business* to buy your services, you're persuading a *person*—a CFO, or a CEO. Take the time to understand *their* core needs. Like any customer, they'll have a problem that you can help solve.

Story codes make every brand communication, from a business pitch to a Superbowl commercial, more compelling and memorable than any other form of marketing. But my Epic Circle framework applies to *every* aspect of marketing. An email. A business statement. Even a customer insight.

In these next examples, I'll demonstrate how to follow and easily put into practice my story framework across six different examples of marketing communication:

1. B2C brand commercial (Samsung)
2. Product commercial (John Lewis & Waitrose)
3. Pitch presentation (Land Rover)
4. Email (TopspinPro)
5. Insight (Durex)
6. Business positioning statement (*The Good the Bad and the Epic*)

****

B2C BRAND COMMERCIAL (2m 30s):
JOHN LEWIS & WAITROSE—EXCITABLE EDGAR

1. **Open with a hook**: We're OUTSIDE in the cold, in a snow-bound Medieval meets fantasy Tudor village. We face two companions—a girl (Ava) and her little green dragon friend (Edgar). The oddness of their friendship hooks us right out of the gates.

2. **Define the problem**: An excitable Edgar is eager to join all the Christmas action: building snowmen and ice-skating. But, in Edgar's enthusiasm, he snorts fire which obviously melts everyone's fun.

3. **Make the brand a guide**: In a way, both the girl and the dragon are mentors to each other. Ava teaches Edgar restraint, while Edgar shows Ava unbridled excitement. Their relationship is also a proxy for the partnership between John Lewis and Waitrose.

4. **Pivot at the mid-point**: The town gathers for their tree unveiling. Ava has wrapped Edgar's mouth shut with a scarf to prevent fire. But this is a false victory.

Edgar shoots flames from his ears and nostrils, burning the Christmas tree down.

5. **Hit a major crisis**: The tree burning is a calamity. He's ruined Christmas. All is lost. Edgar goes into hiding, and Ava plunges into a crisis.

6. **Defeat the villain**: Ava gets an idea to overcome their Outsider Status (the villain). Her plan is to turn Edgar's fire-breathing flaw into a strength and use it to deliver what they've always wanted—acceptance.

7. **Close with a twist**: Edgar and Ava stand INSIDE the warm town hall. Expecting fire, everyone ducks. But here's the twist: Edgar hauls out a pudding and, with a soft snort, sets it to flame. They are welcomed to the feast—transforming from outsiders to insiders.

✳✳✳✳✳✳✳

PRODUCT COMMERCIAL (1m 50s): SAMSUNG—OSTRICH

1. **Open with a hook**: We're looking DOWN on a desert landscape. Below, we see a landlocked flock of flightless birds—ostriches. It's difficult to tell any of them apart in the dust and the heat.

2. **Define the problem**: A female bird breaks from the flock. She arrives at a house and finds a VR headset on a table. Pecking at crumbs, she accidentally puts the headset on and stumbles back in fright.

3. **Make the brand a guide**: Fuelled by the sounds of 'Rocket Man' by Elton John, the flightless bird sees

what it means to fly for the first time. She is transported (by Samsung) into a limitless world.

4. **Pivot at the mid-point**: Her many attempts at lift-off in pursuit of the flock's attention fail spectacularly. At the mid-point, she leaps skyward (the False Victory) ... and crashes into the dirt.

5. **Hit a major crisis**: Our hero finds a secluded place to face her failure. All is lost. The moon rises. She's in The Dark Night of the Soul. Then, she digs deep, spreads her wings and finds a new plan.

6. **Defeat the villain**: Galvanised by soul-searching and without the headset (the mentor has taught her all she needs), she attempts to fly again. This time, she manages somehow to succeed. The flock now pursue *her*. She's no longer a follower. She's defeated the story's villain—CONFORMITY.

7. **Close with a twist**: Our hero achieves what an ostrich can't. She flies. We're looking UP from the desert into the blue limitless sky. Opportunity, independence and freedom loom.

****

PITCH PRESENTATION: LAND ROVER

1. **Open with a hook**: Don't waste time rehashing the brief or writing an agenda. Hit the ground running. Land your theme fast. In our case, it was a unique proposition of *Passionate Expertise*. We introduced it up front as a Cold Open—a pledge to the client.

2. **Define the problem**: Reveal the problem your customer faces. For the Land Rover pitch, we used video to show customers saying how much they loved the brand but how their website failed to meet expectations. We gave a complete summary of the current state, including a description of the current business, consumer and category context. And we gave a detailed description of the desired end state customers wanted from the brand. We then turned that problem into a commercial threat for the business by extrapolating the net cost of inaction.

3. **Make the brand a guide**: Demonstrate how the brand can overcome the customer problem and the process you went through to arrive at a solution. For Land Rover, we laid out the factors that made the brand unique and universally loved.

4. **Pivot at the mid-point**: The set-up argument has been built and the audience is primed for THE BIG IDEA. This is where we landed our Land Rover proposition: *a website that engages with beautifully crafted images and stories of expertise and passion.*

5. **Hit a major crisis**: Unpack all barriers, whether resource, budget, cultural, or tech related. The Major Crisis in this pitch was a lack of resources to deploy premium content that would beat competitors.

6. **Defeat the villain**: Outline the plan to overcome any opposition, including competitor brands—the rivals. The slides here unpack the plan and success metrics. With the Land Rover pitch we built a content delivery platform to meet ambitious deadlines.

7. **Close with a twist**: Drive your message home. In the Land Rover pitch, we ended on a high, presenting a video of the website's *far* vision or desired state. It reflected an inversion of the video content we showcased at the outset of the meeting, which presented the problem. This 'Surprise and Delight' content was a perfect way to end the presentation. It left them primed for a sequel—they wanted more.

****

EMAIL: TOPSPINPRO

TopspinPro is a sports company that develops revolutionary tennis training aids, allowing coaches and players to practice anywhere, anytime. During lockdown, when many firms were battling, TopspinPro saw a surge in sales.

The reason?

Two key factors:

1. **Increased demand for at-home training**: with outdoor activities restricted, tennis players were seeking ways to continue playing and TopspinPro provided the perfect solution for practicing indoors

2. **A story-driven email marketing strategy**: the team shifted from product-centric emails to storytelling—connecting with their audience through relatable content that deepened engagement and grew sales.

The following story-led newsletter released in lockdown, converted to sales at 7.5%. This is compared to the product-led email it replaced which converted at less than 3%.

Subject Line:
Beat those lockdown blues!
Email Header:
TopspinPro energises the Australian Open[1]

Body Copy:
Two weeks ago, 72 players arriving in Melbourne were forced to isolate in hotels around the city. Ellen Perez, ranked 47 in the world, was one of them. She was frustrated. How do you practice tennis in a hotel room?[2]

The next day, videos of pros hitting balls against their mattresses, ands clips of workouts emerged all over the web. So, we snapped into action. We sent free TopspinPros to the prolific posters, like Ellen.[3]

When her TopspinPro arrived, Ellen was excited, but unsure. She didn't know the brand. Would it work?[4] To find out, Ellen first had to unbox the TopspinPro and set it up. The TopspinPro was good to go in under five minutes.[5]

In true Aussie fashion, Ellen posted a few clips. Including one challenging Heather Watson and saying the TopspinPro not only worked but was essential to her Australian Open bid.[6]

I promised to find her some interesting tennis fans from around the world. So, please follow Ellen and let's see if she makes history![7]

1. **Open with a hook**: The subject line is contextual, topical and hyper-relevant, and the header grabs immediate attention. Mental health issues arising from limited time outdoors and living in confined spaces was big news at the time.

2. **Define the problem**: The brand uses a friendly, familiar tone to introduce us to the story's hero and explain the problem Ellen faces. It's a scenario we can all relate to—the frustration and boredom that came with COVID lockdowns

3. **Make the brand a guide**: The brand is introduced as an answer to the problem. TopspinPro lets you practice anywhere, anytime—even in a hotel room. The language used here is simple and to the point. It reflects the brands plucky, positive spirit.

4. **Pivot at the mid-point**: The hero, Ellen, and her problem have been introduced and now the solution arrives in the post. But will Ellen like it?

5. **Hit a major crisis**: It's not objectively a *major* crisis, but TopspinPro *is* honest about the set-up. It doesn't come pre-assembled, so Ellen will have to put the pieces together. It's The IKEA Effect.

6. **Defeat the villain**: We close with success. Ellen loves the product and uses her post to pledge how she intends to beat her key opponent—her rival.

7. **Close with a twist**: The twist isn't blatant, but the ending *is* open and inclusive. Will the TopspinPro keep her game sharp enough to win? *Let's see if she makes history.* The story continues …

****

CUSTOMER INSIGHT

An insight is not a fact. It's not data. It's a customer *truth* that brings a fresh perspective. Epic insights reveal the motivations that lie behind human behaviour.

But the most exciting thing about an insight is this:

A customer insight is a mini story.

What do I mean by that?

Well, any compelling story requires a strong intention and motivation—and a stronger force of opposition. And a good insight articulates exactly that. It might not follow the Seven Story Codes, but it *does* adhere to the Four Essential Elements and the customer (or hero) components of a story:

- **GOAL**: A customer (the hero) wants something (an intention, ambition, or Desire)
- **MOTIVATION**: There's a reason behind why they want it (Need)
- **CONFLICT**: Something—or some*one*—stands in their way (tension or obstacle)

These components (and the solution) are fundamental to any story and every film scene. In fact, if your story isn't working, it's a good bet one of them is missing.

A model that echoes this—and the best technique I've yet found for crafting a customer insight—comes from former P&G Marketing Manager Claire de Belloy Cottier.

It's a powerful approach which may well be inspired by a storytelling guidebook written by Debra Dixon, called *GMC: The Building Blocks of Good Fiction*.

What does **GMC** signify?

You got it:

- Goal[1]
- Motivation[2]
- Conflict[3]

Reflected in de Belloy Cottier's insight structure:

I would like DREAM OR IDEAL SITUATION[1],

because it is important for me to MOTIVATION[2],

but TENSION: WHAT'S BLOCKING THIS[3]?

which leads to the BRAND SOLUTION[4]

Putting it into practice, this Teen audience insight was so clear, a resulting Durex print ad didn't even need a header:

INSIGHT:

I would like to avoid pregnancy when having sex[1],

because I'm not yet ready to have children[2],

but I find that condoms are too expensive[3].

DUREX ANSWER:

Condoms are not expensive, when compared to the cost of a child[4].

The resulting ad?
Just a picture of a condom with a cheap price tag and, alongside it, a stupendously more expensive baby carrier.
Job done.

****

BUSINESS POSITIONING STATEMENT

A **Business Positioning Statement** aims, in as few words as possible, to get people excited about what your business does and the audience you intend to serve. Having a clear positioning statement is useful because it gives any potential customer the ability to understand your offering quickly.

It doesn't have to follow the Seven Story Codes; but it *must* hit the Four Essential Elements of story.

As exemplified in this standard definition:

A Business Positioning explains the target customer segment and their problem, how your brand will help, and the unique plan of action you offer to overcome the core challenges, so that they can succeed.

It easily syncs with my Four Essential Story Elements:

1. The **customer** problem (*the target segment problem*)
2. The **brand** solution (*how your brand will help*)
3. The **obstacles** and Major Crisis (*the unique plan to overcome the core challenges*)
4. The **success** achieved (*so that they can succeed*)

Applied to a story formula, you get this:

CUSTOMER PROBLEM[1]
   +
BRAND SOLUTION[2]
   +
UNIQUE PLAN[3]
   =
SUCCESS[4]

Let's plot this to *The Good the Bad and the Epic*:

IN A CROWDED MARKET, START-UP
BUSINESSES STRUGGLE TO BE HEARD[1].

That's why *The Good the Bad and the Epic* offers a
NARRATIVE STRUCTURE FRAMEWORK[2]

AND SEVEN STORY CODES[3]

Proven to CREATE AND KEEP CUSTOMERS[4].

1. The CUSTOMER PROBLEM identifies a specific
    target segment. In this example, we have ONE hero
    audience in mind. Start-ups.

2. The BRAND SOLUTION is WHAT you intend to
    deliver to solve *their* problem. The product offered
    here is a narrative methodology.

3. The UNIQUE PLAN is HOW you will resolve your
    customer problem like no other brand can. The
    Seven Story Codes offer a unique and simple way to
    overcome *any* marketing challenge.

4. The SUCCESS is your vision for how the brand will
    transform the life of our specific audience.

It's a useful story technique to help you pare back your
business positioning to its essence. And it works for B2B
brands just as well as it does for B2C brands—as shown with
two more examples from the nascent world of AI:

*   EdgeConnect AI
*   Novai

EdgeConnect AI:

Manual portfolio reporting slows decision-making and increases risk for private equity investors and portfolio companies[1]. EdgeConnect solves this by automating data collection and analytics[2] providing a single source of truth for real-time portfolio data[3]. This empowers faster decisions, optimised returns, and better risk assessment[4].

Novai:

Clinicians and researchers struggle with late detection of blindness and neurodegenerative diseases[1] which limits treatment options. Novai overcomes this with AI-driven retinal biomarkers[2]. These are delivered though its unique DARC platform[3], enabling early detection and empowering transformative healthcare to improve patient outcomes[4].

****

HOW TO TAKE THE NEXT STEP

Nine times out of ten brand marketing communications fail because of one thing—they lose the plot. Apply the Epic Circle framework and you're guaranteed to deliver marketing messages that are remembered and shared.

When you sit down to write your business positioning statement or draft a customer insight, use my Four Essential Story Elements to pare them back to the essential.

And when you're writing your next newsletter, crafting your website homepage, or creating your brand origin story, use my Seven Code Framework as a guide:

1. **Open with a hook**: Pledge something interesting to come right from the get-go.

2. **Define the problem**. Evoke emotion by bringing to life your target customer's desires, needs and pain-points—unfiltered and raw.

3. **Make the brand a guide**: Introduce the unique edge your product or service will offer.

4. **Pivot at the mid-point**: Land the solution to the problem. Make this dramatic—a climax.

5. **Hit a major crisis**: Describe how you intend to overcome any setbacks and obstacles.

6. **Defeat the villain**: Show how your brand will use this plan to beat out rivals and achieve success.

7. **Close with a twist**: Leave them wanting more.

The invisible beats of all epic stories are ancient codes that unlock meaning in powerful ways.

Don't lose the plot.

Stick to it.

CHAPTER RECAP

PUTTING IT INTO PRACTICE

The Seven Story Codes of *The Good the Bad and the Epic* apply to every aspect of your marketing. Narrative structure improves everything from a memo to a brand commercial.

Key points to remember:

- **Brand commercial.** Story brands are purpose-led, and a brand commercial must express this purpose in the most compelling way. Brand commercials are the most obvious example of epic storytelling and the easiest format to apply my Seven Story Codes.

- **Product commercial.** Narrative structure can be applied just as effectively to a product commercial. The Samsung *Ostrich* ad is epic. It goes beyond the product to the ultimate benefit the product delivers.

- **Pitch presentation.** A pitch presentation is typically an hour or two long. Storytelling is critical to winning the pitch. You need to hit your plot points to engage and persuade them to buy.

- **Email.** Emails are short stories. You're interrupting someone's day and must earn the right to do that. Give them a story worth reading.

- **Customer Insight.** A customer insight comprises three key elements: goal, motivation, and conflict.

What does the customer want? Why do they want it? What stands in their way? These three elements make every great insight a mini story with an *intention* and an *obstacle*.

- **Business positioning statement**. A good Business Positioning Statement not only defines what you do and where your brand should be positioned in the marketplace, but also the customer segment you aim to target. *The Good the Bad and the Epic's* Four Essential Elements can be instrumental in refining and polishing your business positioning statement, making it easy to understand and compelling. And it's just as effective in the B2B space as it is in B2C.

AFTERWORD

'Not a week goes by that I don't receive
at least one pissed off letter (most
weeks there are more) accusing me of
being foul-mouthed, bigoted,
homophobic, murderous, frivolous or
downright psychopathic.'

– *Stephen King*

Stephen King writes around six pages a day. No matter what life throws at him, he sits down at his desk and writes more than a thousand words every day.

This extraordinary habit has resulted in 200 short stories and over 60 published novels—all bestsellers.

When it comes to understanding story …

King rules.

But even he knows that, as a storyteller, you can't always please everyone. It doesn't matter how many of the Seven Story Codes you adhere to or how many narrative principles you follow; sometimes, for a few, the spark isn't there.

Some stories floor us for the audacity of their message, or for the truth and messiness of a hero's struggle brought to life. But other stories leave us unmoved.

Often—as any author, artist, filmmaker, or marketer will attest—there is no discernible rhyme or reason.

The story simply falls flat.

Why?

According to Rory Sutherland it's because you can never account for the esoteric nature of magic. In his words:

'Not everything that makes sense works, and not everything that works makes sense.'

GO BEYOND GUIDELINES

Storytelling isn't a widget. You can't 'rational' your way to an Oscar, a Pulitzer Prize, or a Cannes Lion. Narrative technique requires expertise, creativity, and, yes, magic.

This is the twist-in-the-tale of my book.

The Good the Bad and the Epic delves into the science and the *art* of storytelling.

It's a head-and-heart approach.

I'm not suggesting you apply an Excel spreadsheet to your brand story, and nor do I forget that creativity often fires unbounded by rules and structure.

No methodology is bulletproof. Of course not.

So, go beyond the guidelines.

But first *understand* them.

Follow the Seven Story Codes, and you'll find a potent force for creating meaning and value.

Picasso mastered formal illustration long before he became the stuff of myth with his cubism. His deep understanding of structure enabled him to *de*construct.

Shakespeare wrote within the constraints of iambic pentameter and five Acts.

Was he a good storyteller?

Eradicate structure from a football or rugby game, and it descends into chaos. The structure is what gives the game meaning. It's the same with a story.

Leave the codes out, and you risk incoherence.

Or, worse, a boring message.

GO BEYOND PROFIT

In the 1980s, Milton Friedman, an economist, argued that businesses have only one responsibility and that was to the shareholder. Big businesses loved this idea because all senior people had whopping share options. Today, the shareholder-only concept has fallen away, and CEOs agree they have a broader stakeholder base to serve:

- Their employees
- Their partners
- The community and society
- But the priority ... is the *customer*

Steve Jobs figured out what matters most to the customer and then designed products like the iPhone and the iPad. In doing so, Apple became the world's first trillion-dollar company. But I'm not some die-hard fanboy. Apple is far from perfect. When they released a tone-deaf ad for the iPad Pro in May 2024, featuring it crushing tools used by creatives, the kickback was immediate and deserved.

It was a gimmick. Not a story.

But, on balance, Apple have used the emotive force of storytelling in positive, exciting, and empowering ways.

This is what I am interested in unlocking—a brand's ability to tap into the emotive force of storytelling to go beyond profit and make a difference in our lives.

And yet, ask people what they define as the purpose of business, and most invariably answer: *'To make money.'*

Economist Ted Levitt disagrees.

> *'Not long ago a lot of companies ... said the purpose [of business] is to make money. But that proved as vacuous as saying that the purpose of life is to eat. Eating is a requisite, not a purpose of life. Without eating, life stops. Profits are a requisite of business. Without profits, business stops.'*
>
> *– Ted Levitt*

In today's world—where financial instability is growing, where the environment is in crisis, and the horrors of war persist—corporations have a broader responsibility to serve.

The once dominant view that companies have only *one* responsibility—to maximise shareholder profit—is built for another time.

Today's brands must go beyond profit.

As Simon Sinek says, they must have a **Just Cause**.

Consider the mountain of data the big four tech brands—Apple, Amazon, Facebook and Google—have on you.

They know you.

They know exactly how to target you with messages that might shock and horrify.

We're all susceptible to doom and gloom. That's why we see so much sensationalism in the media.

Its origin lies in **Negativity Bias**. Which advances that we're more attuned to the bad than the good—a bias that saved our lives when we were hunters and gatherers.

Lion = bad.

Run!

In the wrong hands, marketing messages offer little more than spectacle—grubby tactics engineered to make us chase things we don't really want or need.

But in the right hands, a brand's communication can deliver meaning, authenticity, and genuine value.

Barbie's stellar marketing campaign positioned dolls as more than toys—instead, the dolls represent the limitless possibilities for young girls. A positive campaign idea that spread like wildfire and played a significant part in powering the box-office success of the 2023 film

We see the same dedication to cause with Patagonia.

Just one example of their commitment to environmental concerns was their campaign launched during the Black Friday sales period of 2011.

When all retailers were offering big discounts, Patagonia told shoppers:

Don't buy this jacket.

The idea?

Repair old clothes rather than buying new.

When your brand is ignited with a purpose greater than selling product, you don't just create a brand identity, you create a mythology—exemplified by Joseph Campbell's work, who held that mythology serves four purposes:

1. **The mystical.** Myth helps people express what it feels like to live in awe of the universe.

2. **The cosmological.** Myth allows us to bring order to a messy, complex world. This reflects our ambition to apply logic and meaning to the arcane.

3. **The sociological.** Myth helps establish the rules of a society, helps people live and thrive within them, and makes a difference for others.

4. **The pedagogical.** Finally, Campbell believed that myth helps us create meaning. And this meaning, and the passion it invokes, inspires others.

When they tell their stories effectively, brands tap into and express all four of the purposes of mythology.

By telling their story, brands:

- Become larger than life (doing things others can't)
- Bring order to chaos (using their specific skills)
- Become a role model (standing for something)
- Create meaning (having a purpose)

GO BEYOND BANAL

Highly regarded in the fashion world, Delphine Manivet conjures breath-taking couture. This Parisian dress designer has developed a provocative point of view when it comes to bridalwear. She believes there are few examples in life of brand products that are practical *and* beautiful. So, if a bride's dress is practical, then most likely it's also ugly.

That's not to say her bridal dresses don't have practical considerations. They do of course. But as works of art, the dresses come alive in how they make her brides *feel*.

And how they make the brides' partners feel when they see them in the dress for the first time.

Because *that's* where the essence of the brand lies.

In that look.

It's the story of how they met. Where they fell in love. Their secrets and their history.

All in one look.

On her website homepage, Delphine Manivet has a gem of a positioning statement that speaks directly to this idea and goes to the heart of her brand's mythology.

The line?

It's not a dress. It's a story.

The idea here is easy enough to understand.

The line moves beyond the functional and the material to communicate what the dress means for the wearer and the emotion it provokes in the admirer. It also reflects the care that has gone into imagining and crafting the dress.

The line turns a product into a story about passion and love that transcends the ordinary and the banal.

It turns profane into sacred. As customers we *want* to be part of that transcendence.

We *want* products and brands to be meaningful.

We want them to fit our lives.

Stories give brands provenance.

There's a moment in *Skyfall*, Daniel Craig's third outing as James Bond, where Bond whips back a sheet to reveal his Aston Martin DB5. The scene is just a man looking at a car.

But it's what the silver DB5 represents and who James Bond is—the heft of his mythos—that makes the scene so potent.

We remember Q introducing Sean Connery's Bond to a bullet-proof DB5 in *Goldfinger*. We see Connery leaning coolly against its bodywork in the Swiss Alps.

It's not a car. It's a story.

Compelling stories hold us and don't let go. They reach beyond the banal to deliver value, meaning, and connection.

Story isn't some ancillary part of marketing.

Story *is* marketing.

Your product is a story.

Your customer journey is a story.

Your brand is a story.

And what makes a story compelling?

Narrative structure.

Your brand communication is enriched and made epic by following a framework of narrative beats that are native to us as humans—the Seven Story Codes.

Too many marketing and advertising attempts today, I think we can agree, are insulting. Some constitute nothing more than inane gibberish. We're still force-fed bilge and bullshit.

But epic brands reach beyond.

Epic brands will remain relevant today and into the future because they're **meaningful**—they meet people's needs both functionally and *emotionally*.

They're **different**—they offer things other brands don't.

And they're **salient**—they come to mind quickly at key decision-making moments for customers.

And they do that, by following storytelling codes.

In an age of attention hijacking and brand polyamory, the ability to gain attention and *keep* it is not a nice-to-have; it's a necessity. And with a well-crafted story, it's in your grasp.

Brand marketing and the creative industry is fluid. It will always evolve and pivot to new, more innovative places.

But storytelling is here to stay.

Despite a flood of AI and data-led marketing, storytelling shows no sign of abating. It's more relevant today than ever.

We're all storytellers in this business.

It's what we do.

And when we do it well, we deliver meaning, wonder, and connection in ways that nothing else can.

With *The Good the Bad and the Epic* I'm not proposing something revolutionary. All I'm saying is make content that people choose. People don't choose marketing messages.

They choose emotion. They choose meaning.

They choose stories.

It comes down to this:

If you're looking to make your brand epic …
If you aim to communicate with more impact …
If you want to *create* and *keep* customers …

There's only one proven method.
Tell them a story.

ACKNOWLEDGEMENTS

*'The weapon of mass attraction is the
ability to communicate ... Money,
mates, and meaning are all moths to the
flame of storytelling.'*

— *Scott Galloway*

We ride on the shoulders of giants in life. A truth I've never felt more profoundly than in compiling the content for *The Good the Bad and the Epic*. Without my wise mentors and allies, hardly a page would remain.

The seed for the book was planted when I presented alongside John Yorke in 2019. His storytelling analysis in *Into the Woods* is pure genius. Many scholars of Dramatic Structure and Narrative Technique have inspired me:

Joseph Campbell. Jill Chamberlain. Lee Child. Alfonso Cuarón. Debra Dixon. Syd Field. Gustav Freytag. Bernadette Jiwa. Dan Harmon. Stephen King. David Mamet. Robert McKee. Philip Pullman. Blake Snyder. Andrew Stanton. John Truby. Christopher Vogler. Kurt Vonnegut.

I owe a debt to the gods of marketing too.

Rory Sutherland is a colleague and a TED legend. No one alive is a more accomplished brand raconteur.

I thank the icons of science, business and philosophy:

Jennifer Aaker. Jeff Bezos. Jerome Bruner. Stuart Butterfield. Andy Clark. James Clear. Jim Collins. Claire de Belloy Cottier. Jules Ehrhardt. Nir Eyal. John Fahy. Carmine Gallo. Scott Galloway. Malcolm Gladwell. Seth Godin. David Jobber. Steve Jobs. Daniel Kahneman. Phil Knight. Arthur Koestler. Steve Krug. Ted Levitt. Josh Linkner. Margaret Mark. Donald Miller. Satya Nadella. Peg Neuhauser. Carol Pearson. Barry Schwartz. Simon Sinek. Gerald Zaltman. Bluma Zeigarnik.

I hope they won't feel I've borrowed, but rather that I've honoured and built on their ideas.

I'm grateful for my talented colleagues through the years. Agitators, free spirits, and firebrands all of them:

Melissa Allwork. Chris Averill. Omar Bakhshi. Dominic Bates. James Bell. Sarah Blackman. Jesse Bouman. Nick Brackenbury. Harriet Bradley. James Chadwick. Thorkild Clausen. Alex Cussell. Ed Cox. Claire Dale. Dayoán Daumont. Beth Ann Eliason-Lim. Melanie Elliot. Kailas Elmer. Andy Feasey. Katherine Francis. Isabel Fonte. Fiona Gordon. Kate Gowers. Mirko Grahnert. Dave Green. Chris Greywoode. Lucy Hamilton. Rik Haslam. Ann Higgins. Roger Horrocks. Nick Howell. Jacob Hudson. David Hughes. David Jacques. Noor Jafar. Brian Jensen. Shailen Joshi. Gavin King. Tim Kitchener. Rajus Korde. Clare Lawson. Lindsay Landy. Matthew Leem. Mary Lloyd. Matthew Lucas. Scott McKinnon. Serge Millbank. Aurel Moussa. James Myers. Colin Nimick. Patou Nuytemans. Sevil Ozer Crespo. Chip Peterson. Jan Piatkowski. Alison Price. Hamish Priest. Damayanti Purkayastha. Sean Rach. John Reardon. Giles Rhys Jones. Ben Richards. Olivia Rzepczynski Clasper. Erika Santonastaso. Brian Sassoon. Isabel Schnell. John Shaw. Andy Smith. Kush Thakrar. Keith Timimi. Anna Vogt. Matt Watkinson. Julian Watt. Rob Wells. Kate Wheaton. Ryan Wylie. And so many more.

Finally, my storytelling friends and family:

Alan Alston. Julia Boggio. Clare Buttery. Sean Cash. Zoë Crookes. Mel Darbon. Glen Drysdale. Clare Furniss. Darren Giblin. Bruce Good. Julia Green. Anna Jean Hart. Finbar Hawkins. Lu Hersey. Michael Hodge. Dianne Hofmeyr. Michael Hofmeyr. Phillip Hofmeyr. Beverly Horowitz. Ben Horslen. Marc Kahn. Charlotte Lambkin. Delphine Manivet. Alessandro Sacerdote. Daniel Scherl. Helenka Stachera. Antonella Strömberg. Mimi Thebo. Stephanie Thwaites. Chris Vick. Steve Voake. Tig Wallace.

Every story must have mentors and allies.

These are mine.

Thank you for your expertise, trust and care.

And to *you*, the reader and real guru, I can't wait to hear the powerful story you will unleash on the world.

An epic brand story no one else can tell.

Yours.

REFERENCES

CHAPTER ONE

- Aristotle (2013) *Poetics*. Translated by Anthony Kenny. Oxford University Press.
- Ehrhardt, J. (2019). *Samsung launching narcissism into space is everything wrong with marketing today.* Campaign US. https://www.campaignasia.com/article/samsung-launching-narcissism-into-space-is-everything-wrong-with-marketing-today/455137
- Eyal, N. (2013) *Hooked: How to Build Habit-Forming Products.* Random House.
- Gallo, C. (2014). *Talk Like TED: The 9 Public Speaking Secrets of the World's Top Minds.* Macmillan.
- Leo Burnett Chicago (2018). Samsung *Ostrich.* https://www.dandad.org/awards/professional/2018/film-advertising/26574/ostrich-samsung/
- Schwartz, B. (2004). *The Paradox of Choice: Why More Is Less.* Harper Perennial.
- Snow, S. (2023). *Science Shows: Humans Have Massive Capacity For Sustained Attention, And Storytelling Unlocks It.* Forbes. https://www.forbes.com/sites/shanesnow/2023/01/16/science-shows-humans-have-massive-capacity-for-sustained-attention-and-storyte ling-unlocks-it/
- Stevenson, B. (2012). *We need to talk about injustice.* TED Talks. https://www.ted.com/talks/bryan_stevenson_we_need_to_talk_about_an_injustice?
- Tracksuit & TikTok. (2024). *The Awareness Advantage.*

https://www.gotracksuit.com/uk/report/the-awareness-advantage

CHAPTER TWO

- Bruner, J. (1986). *Actual Minds, Possible Worlds* (The Jerusalem-Harvard Lectures). Harvard University Press.
- Campbell, J. (1949). *The Hero with a Thousand Faces.* 1st edition, Bollingen Foundation.
- Eisenstadt, L. (2005) *Empathy on the Brain.* Boston University. https://www.bu.edu/sjmag/scimag2005/features/mirrorneurons.htm
- Gallo, C. (2014). *The Maya Angelou Quote That Will Radically Improve Your Business.* Forbes. https://www.forbes.com/sites/carminegallo/2014/05/31/the-maya-angelou-quote-that-will-radically-improve-your-business/
- Gibney, A. Documentary (2015). *Steve Jobs: The Man in the Machine.* CNN Films. Jigsaw Productions. Magnolia.
- Grossman, D. (2021). *The Power of Storytelling.* https://www.yourthoughtpartner.com/blog/bid/75117/the-power-of-storytelling
- Huddleston, G., & Rocha, S. (2018). *Don Draper, Teacher-as-Artist: A Diffractive Reading of Mad Men.* Taboo: The Journal of Culture and Education. https://doi.org/10.31390/taboo.17.3.05
- Keating, G. (2013). *Netflixed: The Epic Battle for America's Eyeballs.* Penguin.
- Levitt, T. (1983). *The Marketing Imagination.* Macmillan.
- Mizerak, J. (2023). *Is the Rise of AI the Fall of Storytelling?* PaperplaneCo.

https://www.paperplaneco.com/blog/is-the-rise-of-ai-the-fall-of-storytelling/
- Neuhauser, P. (1993). *Corporate Legends and Lore: The Power of Storytelling as a Management Tool*. McGraw-Hill Inc., US.
- Snow, S., & Lazauskas, J. (2018). *The Storytelling Edge: How to Transform Your Business, Stop Screaming into the Void, and Make People Love You*. Wiley.
- Smith, B. (2020). *1917 Screenplay Analysis*. Monument.
  https://monumentscripts.com/1917-screenplay-analysis/
- Sutherland, R. (2019). *Alchemy: The Surprising Power of Ideas that Don't make Sense*. Penguin.
- Vogler, C. (2020). *The Writer's Journey: Mythic Structure for Writers*. 25th Anniversary. Michael Wiese Productions.
- Zak, P.J. (2014). *Why Your Brain Loves Good Storytelling*. Harvard Business Review.
  https://hbr.org/2014/10/why-your-brain-loves-good-storytelling

CHAPTER THREE

- Sontag, S. (2007). *At the Same Time: Essays and Speeches*. Picador.

CHAPTER FOUR

- Daddona, M. (2018). *Got Milk? How the iconic campaign came to be, 25 years ago*. Fast Company.
  https://www.fastcompany.com/40556502/got-milk-how-the-iconic-campaign-came-to-be-25-years-ago

- Gladwell, M. (2006). *Blink: The Power of Thinking Without Thinking*. Penguin.
- Jobs, S. (2007). Introducing the iPhone at Macworld in San Francisco. CNET Highlights. https://www.youtube.com/watch?v=9hYjzF3OJyMDfvsd
- Masterclass (2021). *How to Use Antithesis in Your Writing: Definition and Examples of Antithesis as a Literary Device* https://www.masterclass.com/articles/how-to-use-antithesis-in-your-writing
- Masterclass (2021). *Cold Opens Explained: How to Write a Cold Open*. https://www.masterclass.com/articles/what-is-a-cold-open
- Sawhney, V. (2020). *Why Your Brain Dwells on Unfinished Tasks*. Harvard Business Review.
- Snyder, B. (2005). *Save The Cat: The last Book on Screenwriting That You'll Ever Need*. Michael Wiese Productions.
- Stanton, A. (2012). *The Clues to a Great Story*. TED Talks. https://www.ted.com/talks/andrew_stanton_the_clues_to_a_great_story
- Ulloa, A. & Landekic, L. (2015). *Raging Bull (1980)*. Art of the Title. https://www.artofthetitle.com/title/raging-bull/
- Vonnegut, K. (1999). *Bagombo Snuff Box: Uncollected Short Fiction*. Putnam.
- Wikipedia. *The Inverted Pyramid* (Journalism). https://en.wikipedia.org/wiki/Inverted_pyramid_(journalism)

CHAPTER FIVE

- Bariso, J. (2020). *Steve Jobs' Incredible Lesson on How to Respond Perfectly To Any Insult*. Thrive Global. https://community.thriveglobal.com/steve-jobs-incredible-lesson-on-how-to-respond-perfectly-to-any-insult/
- Child, L. (2019). *The Hero*. TLS Books.
- Doran, G. T. (1981). *There's a S.M.A.R.T. Way to Write Management's Goals and Objectives*. Management Review, Vol. 70, Issue 11, pp. 35-36.
- Gladwell, M. (2004). *Choice, Happiness, and Spaghetti Sauce*. TED Talks. https://www.ted.com/talks/malcolm_gladwell_choice_happiness_and_spaghetti_sauce
- Jobs, S. (1997). Worldwide Developer Conference in Cupertino. https://www.systemiks.com/cries-and-whispers-a-lesson-in-communication-from-steve-jobs/
- Krznaric, R. (2015). *Empathy: Why It Matters, and How to Get It*. Tarcherperigee.
- Koestler, A. (1968). *The Ghost in the Machine: The urge to self-destruction: a psychological and evolutionary study of modern man's predicament*. MacMillan.
- Leo Burnett Chicago (2018). Samsung *Ostrich*. https://www.dandad.org/awards/professional/2018/film-advertising/26574/ostrich-samsung/
- Lev-Ram, M. (2017). *Microsoft CEO Satya Nadella Says Empathy Makes You a Better Innovator*. Fortune. https://fortune.com/2017/10/03/microsoft-ceo-satya-nadella-says-empathy-makes-you-a-better-innovator/

- Murphy Jr., B. (2023). *Jeff Bezos: The Most Important Single Thing is to Focus Obsessively on the Customer*. INC.
  https://www.inc.com/bill-murphy-jr/bezos-most-important-single-thing-focus-obsessively-on-customer.html
- Nadella, S. (2017). *Hit Refresh. The Quest to Rediscover Microsoft's Soul and Imagine a Better Future for Everyone*. Harper Business.
- Reill, A. (2023). *A Simple Way to Make Better Decisions*. Harvard Business Review. https://hbr.org/2023/12/a-simple-way-to-make-better-decisions
- Rock, D. (2008). *SCARF: A Brain-Based Model for Collaborating With and Influencing Others*. Neuroleadership Journal, 1, 1-9.
- Truby, J. (2008). *The Anatomy of Story: 22 Steps to Becoming a Master Storyteller*. Farrar, Straus and Giroux.
- Zaltman, G. (2003). *How Customers Think: Essential Insights into the Mind of the Market*. Harvard Business Review Press.

CHAPTER SIX

- Burke, S. (2007). *Trust in leadership: A multi-level review and integration*. The Leadership Quarterly 18 606-632.
- Clark, A. (2023). *The Experience Machine: How Our Minds Predict and Shape Reality*. Allen Lane.
- Collins, J. (2001). *Good To Great: Why Some Companies Make The Leap … And Others Don't*. Random House Business.

- Gladwell, M. (2006). *Blink: The Power of Thinking Without Thinking*. Penguin.
- Gladwell, M., & Galhotra, K., in conversation with Guay, R. (2021). https://www.youtube.com/watch?v=VObEKZh-Weg
- Godin. S. (2018). *This is Marketing: You Can't be Seen Until You learn to See*. Penguin.
- Hart, R. (2018). *Brands Must Keep Their Promises With Customer Experience (CX)*. Forrester. https://www.forrester.com/blogs/brands-must-keep-their-promises-with-customer-experience-cx/
- Jobber, D., & Fahy, J. (2022). *Foundations of Marketing. Seventh Edition*. McGraw Hill.
- Krug, S. (2000). *Don't Make Me Think! A Common Sense Approach to Web Usability*. New Riders.
- Mamet, D. (2017). *David Mamet teaches dramatic Writing*. Masterclass. https://www.masterclass.com/classes/david-mamet-teaches-dramatic-writing
- Mark, M., & Pearson, C. (2001). *The Hero and The Outlaw: Building Extraordinary Brands Through the Power of Archetypes*. McGraw-Hill.
- Milgram, S. (1963). *Behavioural Study of Obedience*. Journal of Abnormal and Social Psychology.
- Sutherland, R. (2019). *Alchemy: The Surprising Power of Ideas that Don't make Sense*. Penguin.
- VandeHei, J., & Allen, M., & Schwartz, R. (2023). *Smart Brevity: The Power of Saying More with Less*. Nicholas Brealey Publishing.
- Wason, P. (1960). *On the failure to eliminate hypotheses in a conceptual task*. Quarterly Journal of Experimental Psychology.
- Watkinson, M. (2012). *Mastering Uncertainty: the ten Principles behind Great Customer Experiences*. Ft Press

CHAPTER SEVEN

- Adam & Eve / DDB (2019). John Lewis & Waitrose. *Excitable Edgar.* https://www.youtube.com/watch?v=AzIT3pbbZr8
- Campbell, J. (1949). *The Hero with a Thousand Faces.* 1st edition, Bollingen Foundation.
- The Chartered Institute of Marketing (2019). *The secrets of John Lewis's Christmas success.* https://www.cim.co.uk/content-hub/editorial/the-secrets-of-john-lewiss-christmas-success/
- Freytag, G. (2004). *Technique of the Drama: An Exposition of Dramatic Composition and Art.* University Press of the Pacific.
- Gladwell, M. (2004). *Choice, Happiness, and Spaghetti Sauce.* TED Talks. https://www.ted.com/talks/malcolm_gladwell_choice_happiness_and_spaghetti_sauce
- Johnson, R. (2019). *Crafting the Perfect Plot Twist.* IMDB. https://www.imdb.com/title/tt11469160/?ref_=tt_mv_close
- Leo Burnett Chicago (2018). Samsung *Ostrich.* https://www.dandad.org/awards/professional/2018/film-advertising/26574/ostrich-samsung/
- Miley, J. (2018). *This Surfer Was Awarded the Guinness World Record for the Biggest Wave Ever Surfed.* Interesting Engineering. https://interestingengineering.com/video/this-surfer-was-awarded-the-guinness-world-record-for-the-biggest-wave-ever-surfed
- Puzo, M. (2012). *The Godfather.* Cornerstone.

- Snyder, B. (2005). *Save The Cat: The last Book on Screenwriting That You'll Ever Need*. Michael Wiese Productions.
- Thomas, D. (2019) *Christmas adverts – do they really work?* BBC News. https://www.bbc.co.uk/news/business-50392008
- Yorke, J. (2013). *Into the Woods: How Stories Work and Why We Tell Them*. Penguin Random House UK.

CHAPTER EIGHT

- Adam & Eve / DDB (2019). John Lewis & Waitrose. *Excitable Edgar*. https://www.youtube.com/watch?v=AzIT3pbbZr8
- Bonnet, D., & Buvat, J., & Subrahmanyam, K.V.J. (2017) *When Digital Disruption Strikes: How Can Incumbents Respond?* Capgemini Consulting. https://www.capgemini.com/consulting/wp-content/uploads/sites/30/2017/07/digital_disruption_1.pdf
- Cialdini, R. (2007). *Influence: The Psychology of Persuasion*. HarperBus.
- Clark, K. (2019). *The Slack origin story: How a whimsical online game became an enterprise software giant*. TechCrunch. https://techcrunch.com/2019/05/30/the-slack-origin-story/
- Coldeway, D. (2020). *We've come full rectangle: Polaroid is reborn out of The Impossible Project*. TechCrunch. https://techcrunch.com/2020/03/27/weve-come-full-rectangle-polaroid-is-reborn-out-of-the-impossible-project/
- McConaughey, M. (2023). *Greenlights*. Headline.

- Kuperman, B. *On Volkswagen and "Think Small".* https://www.youtube.com/watch?v=SwWJIjWfC0M&t =67s
- Randolph, E. (2017). *Storytelling: It's about Going Primal*. Jami Gold. https://jamigold.com/2017/12/storytelling-its-about-going-primal-guest-elizabeth-randolph/
- Shotton, R. (2018). *The Choice Factory: 25 behavioural biases that influence why we buy.* Harriman House Ltd.
- Shotton, R. (2018). *If you want to earn consumers' love, flaunt your flaws*. Marketing Week. https://www.marketingweek.com/richard-shotton-consumer-love-flaunt-flaws/
- Snyder, B. (2005). *Save The Cat: The last Book on Screenwriting That You'll Ever Need*. Michael Wiese Productions.
- Wang, R. (2015). *Disrupting Digital Business: Create an Authentic Experience in the Peer-to-Peer Economy.* Harvard Business Review Press.
- Wilson, P. and Rebeiro, M. (2021) *Turning defence into attack: How Formula E built a new fanbase by embracing its biggest weakness*. WARC. https://www.warc.com/content/paywall/article/APG/ Turning_defence_into_attack_How_Formula_E_built_ a_new_fanbase_by_embracing_its_biggest_weakness/

CHAPTER NINE

- Adams, P. (2022). *How Coke and Pepsi's rivalry shaped marketing—and where it goes next*. MarketingDive. https://www.marketingdive.com/news/coke-vs-pepsi-rivalry-brand-marketing-metaverse/621711/
- Coca-Cola (2016). *Share a Coke: How The Groundbreaking Campaign Got Its Start 'Down Under'.*

https://www.coca-cola.com/au/en/media-center/share-a-coke-how-the-groundbreaking-campaign-got-its-start-down-under

- Jaffe, E. (2014). *How Apple's Famous "I'm a Mac" ads Branded Fanboys For Life.* Fast Company. https://www.fastcompany.com/91016143/best-jobs-2024-good-salaries-flexible-wfh-indeed-list
- O'Hara, C. (2014). *How to Tell a Great Story.* Harvard Business Review. https://hbr.org/2014/07/how-to-tell-a-great-story
- Seery, B. (2019). *#OrchidsandOnions: BMW's Benz stunt stuns.* BizCommunity. https://www.bizcommunity.com/Article/196/12/191458.html
- Snyder, B. (2005). *Save The Cat: The last Book on Screenwriting That You'll Ever Need.* Michael Wiese Productions.
- Sutherland, R. (2019). *Alchemy: The Surprising Power of Ideas that Don't make Sense.* Penguin
- TBWA Media Arts Lab (2006-2009). Apple *I'm a Mac* Campaign. https://www.youtube.com/watch?v=qfv6Ah_MVJU
- Truby, J. (2008). *The Anatomy of Story: 22 Steps to Becoming a Master Storyteller.* Farrar, Straus and Giroux.
- VML (2024) *Thanks for Coke-Creating: Embracing local culture and creativity through iconic branding.* https://www.vml.com/work/every-coca-cola-is-welcome

CHAPTER TEN

- Adam & Eve / DDB (2019). John Lewis & Waitrose. *Excitable Edgar.*

https://www.youtube.com/watch?v=AzIT3pbbZr8
- Forsman & Bodenfors (2017). Volvo. *Moments.*
  https://www.youtube.com/watch?v=AM-2HlgPftE&t=205s
- Kahneman, D. (2010). *The riddle of experience vs memory.* TED Talks.
  https://www.ted.com/talks/daniel_kahneman_the_riddle_of_experience_vs_memory?language=en
- Kahneman, D. (2012). *Thinking, Fast and Slow.* Penguin.
- Kermode, M. (1967). *Sense of an Ending: Studies in the Theory of Fiction.* Oxford University Press
- Leo Burnett Chicago (2018). Samsung *Ostrich.*
  https://www.dandad.org/awards/professional/2018/film-advertising/26574/ostrich-samsung/
- Masterclass (2016). Aaron *Sorkin Teaches Screenwriting.*
  https://www.masterclass.com/classes/aaron-sorkin-teaches-screenwriting
- Sinek, S. (2009). *Start with Why: How Great Leaders Inspire Everyone to Take Action.* Portfolio.
- Snyder, B. (2005). *Save The Cat: The last Book on Screenwriting That You'll Ever Need.* Michael Wiese Productions.
- Titz, D. & Lebherz, D. (2015). Johnnie Walker *Dear Brother.*
  https://www.youtube.com/watch?v=h2caT4q4Nbs&t=4s

CHAPTER ELEVEN

- Adam & Eve / DDB (2019). John Lewis & Waitrose. *Excitable Edgar.*

- Anomaly (2015). Budweiser. *Lost Dog.*
  https://www.youtube.com/watch?v=JRxgiRGfbC8
- de Belloy Cottier, C. and de Belloy, A. (2016). LEFT Productions.
  https://www.linkedin.com/pulse/multinationals-secret-creating-extremely-powerful-claire-de-belloy/
- Dixon, D. (2013). *GMC: Goal, Motivation, and Conflict: The Building Blocks of Good Fiction.* Bell Bridge Books.
- Ladd, B. (2022). *Why And How Every Company Should Use Amazon's Six-Page Memo Format.* Forbes.
  https://www.forbes.com/sites/forbescommunications council/2022/08/30/why-and-how-every-company-should-use-amazons-six-page-memo-format/
- Leo Burnett Chicago (2018). Samsung *Ostrich.*
  https://www.dandad.org/awards/professional/2018/film-advertising/26574/ostrich-samsung/
- Quesenberry, K. A., & Coolsen, M. K. (2014). *What Makes a Super Bowl Ad Super? Five-Act Dramatic Form Affects Consumer Super Bowl Advertising Ratings.* Journal of Marketing Theory and Practice, 22(4), 437–454.
  https://doi.org/10.2753/MTP1069-6679220406
- Rosen, J. (2014). *Super Bowl ads: Stories beat sex and humor, Johns Hopkins researcher finds.* John Hopkins University Hub.
  https://hub.jhu.edu/2014/01/31/super-bowl-ads/
- Yorke, J. (2013). *Into the Woods: How Stories Work and Why We Tell Them.* Penguin Random House UK.

CHAPTER TWELVE

- Bali, K. (2023). *Joyconomy: Where Brands Are The Architects Of Our Happiness.* Creative Salon.

https://creative.salon/articles/features/brands-delivering-optimism-and-joy-wunderman-thompson

- Campbell, J. (1949). *The Hero with a Thousand Faces*. 1st edition, Bollingen Foundation.
- Galloway, S. (2023). *Storytelling*. No Mercy / No Malice Newsletter. https://medium.com/@profgalloway/storytelling-64944222b43#
- King, S. (2001). *On Writing: A Memoir of the Craft*. Hodder.
- Levitt, T. (1983). *The Marketing Imagination*. Macmillan.
- Mamet, D. (2017). *David Mamet teaches dramatic Writing*. Masterclass. https://www.masterclass.com/classes/david-mamet-teaches-dramatic-writing
- Sinek, S. (2019). *The Infinite Game*. Penguin Business.

LIST OF ILLUSTRATIONS

Dramatic Composition and Art. University Press of the Pacific.

p. 156   Figure 10: YIN-YANG AND THE SEVEN STORY CODES. © David Hofmeyr.

p. 180   Figure 11: THE PEAK-END RULE. Adapted from Kahneman, D. (2010). *The riddle of experience vs memory.* TED Talks.

INDEX